PRAISE FOR
The Male Manifesto

"The Dalai Lama said "My religion is simple. My religion is kindness" and again "Happiness is not something readymade. It comes from our own actions." Rick Morgenstern, in his book The Male Manifesto digs deep into his own spiritual roots to present a path to happiness for young men willing to do the work. It is a path that will help these young men grow up to live a life of accountability, authenticity and integrity as well as to wake up to a vision of personal mission in service to the world. There is little doubt that what this world needs is more grown up, wide awake men. Kudos to Rick for his work on this book."
– Kodo Michael Elser, Priest, Integral Zen, Hollow Bones; Past Chair, ManKind Project USA

"Starting from "the plight of the American male," arising from his personal experiences of love, fatherhood, life, loss and transformation, and informed by his worldview and ongoing learnings, Rick Morgenstern provides a compelling charge for the reclamation of male connection. The Male Manifesto reaches out and asks us all to recognize the wide gap between the degree of connection to self that men need and that which is present at large in the culture today, with clear guidance and suggestions of steps men can take to bridge that expanse."

– Jon Levitt, Managing Member, JSA Business Development

"I have worked with Rick Morgenstern for the last eight years in the leadership of the ManKind Project. What I've watched him do has been pivotal in developing and bringing forward the entire system of our men's circles on a national level. We wouldn't be where we are in the quality of men's work in our weekly small groups without his leadership. I've also witnessed and experienced the work Rick has done with men one on one, helping them find ways to access and heal their deep wounds. Rick has become a close personal friend of mine as a result of the depth of who he is, his love and joy that just is who he is, and how he expresses it all the time. It's obvious to me in the work I'm involved in that men, especially young men, are searching for all resources possible to help work through the parts of themselves that need to grow up so that they can be, and experience, healthy masculinity. This book, The Male Manifesto, offers the opportunity for men to be able to see and work on those parts of themselves. My hope is you'll read this book and grow in yourself as I have grown."

– Paul Samuelson, Former Mayor, Langley, WA; Current Chair – ManKind Project USA

"I am deeply grateful for the bond I share with Rick Morgenstern. His wisdom, commitment and love are my steadfast companions as I walk my path through this life. I am so pleased that Rick is now making this gift available to anyone willing to open up and receive it. The Male Manifesto is exactly the wisdom needed right now as men struggle to understand how to grow up and live a life of true integrity. These clear words of truth have the power to change your life forever; you need to read this book!"

– Greg Simon, Senior Technical Specialist, 3M

"I've been doing "men's work" for more than 20 years, and consumed a ton of books, articles, podcasts, lectures, blogs etc. about what it means to be a man. But if I had to recommend just one book on the topic to start — this is it. Rick Morgenstern's The Male Manifesto is a highly readable yet profoundly rich guide for men who are ready to change their lives for the better. Full disclosure: I've "sat" with Rick in a men's group for the past three years, consider him a true friend, and would love to see this book become a best-seller. So maybe I'm biased. What I know for sure is that he is an incredible man with great heart and wisdom, and this book is a reflection of that. I think it will change people's lives."

– Mitch Teplitsky - Filmmaker and Communications Consultant

CONTENTS

Foreword .... *x*
Preface .... *xii*
Introduction .... *xiii*

Chapter One: The Plight of the American Male 1

Chapter Two: The Emasculated Male 11

Chapter Three: Male Initiation in Other Cultures 31

Chapter Four: Living a Virtuous Life 43

Chapter Five: Today's Self-Actualized Man 55

Chapter Six: A Hero's Journey 69

Chapter Seven: Conclusion 85

Paradigms 87
Ground Rules 92
Acknowledgements 95

To the memory of

Fritz Morgenstern,

the finest bus driver I ever knew

FOREWORD

Learning how to cultivate mature masculinity is one of this century's most crucial challenges. Any words of wisdom spoken clearly and convincingly on this challenge are welcome as sunrise.

So, I am heartened to read and eager to commend this work on male maturity by Rick Morgenstern. I have shared enough of life's journey with him to know he speaks from a deeply authentic and soulful experience of the risks and rewards of masculine initiation.

His book contains the story of how he discovered deeper wisdom about masculine wholeness. It begins with the perception that most men of his acquaintance were full-blown adolescents in full-grown male bodies. He discovered this was true of his own beloved father and consequently also of himself.

His attempts to establish himself as a man included experiencing the ecstasy of business success and the agony of its failure. He encountered the same fateful cycle in his relational life. He moved through high romance and loving marriage to a deteriorating relationship and ultimate divorce.

In this time of deep trial, his transformation began. He discovered the secret of surrender — the surrender of his egocentric style of life and the opening of himself to the resources of spiritual living and masculine initiation.

Among the resources he discovered was a vital, ongoing, caring male community. In this community men dedicated themselves to helping one another find a new way of becoming a mature, noble, consciously self-giving man.

He has now become, as his readers will soon discover, a wise teacher who is willing to share his vision of how one's own life can be transformed into the richness of mature masculine energy capable of blessing the world.

— Don Jones
Full Leader, Former Chairman, Seminal Visionary: The ManKind Project Author of Wisdom for the Journey

PREFACE

This little book is about change. It is about an expanded paradigm of living, for men. It is about making connections that run deep inside. It is about discovering one's truth. It is about maturity, and virtue. It is about being exceptionally human.

In writing this book I bring my own biases to bear. Bias is a fundamental condition of being human: it goes with the territory. Proclaiming a position of non-bias as a writer is the same as proclaiming a position of non-truth. We are each one of us an amalgamation of child-rearing, socialization, and genetic makeup. With all that comes individual perspective, and with individual perspective comes bias. I make no apology for my own biases, and I also make conscious attempts to temper them with non-judgment, compassion, and tolerance. For me, that is the healthiest approach to writing, and to living life.

I'm presenting this book to a very specific audience: males who are married to women or intend to be married to women, who have children or intend to have children, and who have an abiding desire to experience relationship with God. I have selected this particular group because I was raised to be a male with these conditions applied in my life. As such, I know the audience well. Other audiences, while just as valid as this one, are audiences I don't know, so I will not attempt to address them in these writings.

INTRODUCTION

In the spring of 2009 my father — Fritz Morgenstern, 81 years old — committed suicide. It took him 16 years to complete the task. His suicide was spiritual in nature, and his body just went along for the ride. I watched it happen. The time has come for me to tell the story of his life.

Dad was one of those guys — we all know the type — who folks described as "They threw away the mold when they made that one." Fritz Morgenstern lit up a room when he was in his prime: a natural born leader and a real character, a man who never met a stranger. Dad was my greatest hero. I miss him every day of my life. He inspired me to be the best person I can be; that was his gift to me as his son.

I have written The Male Manifesto to honor this noble man Fritz Morgenstern, and to impart the learning I derived from the source of his anguish as a man. My father was one of the noblest men I've ever had the privilege of knowing, yet he was a man who stopped growing up when he reached his teenage years. To be honest, my father was an emotional impotent, especially toward the end of his life. He was stuck at the age of 18 inside, in his innermost parts, for his entire life. He died an emotional impotent.

Unwittingly, and thoroughly, my father taught his son, me, how to be an emotional impotent, just like him. I witnessed it every day of my life as a boy growing up. It took almost 40 years of my own living, including deep emotional trial along with profound inner work to unlearn how to be a full-grown immature man and teach myself the essence of male maturity. I arrived at that juncture somewhat over a decade and a half ago. The difference in me between then and now has been nothing short of transformational.

I know what it feels like to live both ways — stuck adolescent vs. mature man — and let me tell you life as a mature man is akin to relaxing on a raft in calm water compared to the alternative. Using my maturity as a guidepost I feel practically unstoppable in my desire to make a positive difference to those around me, and to the world. I feel, daily, that I have truly arrived as a man. That is a profound gift; I feel so blessed to have received it. God brought it; only by the Grace of God do I have it.

Maturity is half of the puzzle in the makeup of a healthy man. What good is maturity in a man who lives without virtue, who lives with evil in his life? Maturity can be used to create evil just as effectively as it can to create good, and evil is not healthy. In my experience, it takes both maturity and nobility to make a healthy man. Just as a man can be mature in his consciousness and evil in his behavior, so too can a man be adolescent in his consciousness and noble in his behavior. Either one of these scenarios causes a man to be un-whole and incomplete. In my father's life the latter scenario was true. Dad acted as a role model of emotional impoverishment for me. At the same time he acted as a role model of virtue; he practiced noble behavior and held noble intentions in life.

I learned from my father at an early age the

essence of the Golden Rule, witnessing his gifts to fellow humans in countless gestures of kindness. I learned from my father's noble behavior for decades, and it over time sunk into the fabric of my being. As a man I proudly carry his legacy of living a noble life, and I continually look for opportunities to teach those principles to anyone who might be receptive to them, especially the youth. It is a lifelong pursuit of mine. It is the best way I can honor the memory of my father.

This legacy, as incredible as it is to me, makes the tragedy of his emotional immaturity difficult for me to reconcile, because I see now that it takes both emotional maturity and noble living to make a whole and complete man. Dad figured out half of the puzzle, but he never made it all the way. I wish with all my heart that he would have made it all the way. That was not meant to be.

The story of the last several years of my father's life is a tragic one to me because he simply checked himself out of the game. After 50 some years of giving, he was spent. Fritz Morgenstern had no more to give; he had entirely used himself up. He had taken on so much in life (so much of other people's baggage — he was a career caregiver), and had never taught himself how to emotionally handle life as a mature man, that by retirement age the well had simply run dry. During his elder years, at the very time he should have shown like a diamond, radiant in his fathering and blessing wisdom, he in reality allowed himself to turn into a lump of coal. He was not present any longer for his wife, for his children, or for his grandchildren. He gave little to nothing to the larger community. Everyone close to him desired his wisdom and his blessing, but he just couldn't bring himself to give those gifts. The tragedy was that during countless opportunities at the end of his life he chose to withhold his insight and his blessing. Everyone who knew him well and knew what he was made of saw this happen. I think, silently (even openly at times) we all shared that tragedy together. I certainly felt it profoundly as his son. This was not the man who raised me; that man gave entirely of himself.

When I was a young boy, growing up with my father, the church was our second home, dad being a pastor. I remember many an evening falling asleep on a church pew during choir practice. Dad had the entrepreneurial spirit about him as do many active pastors, in my experience. He had vision, and ambition, and a knack for using limited resources to their fullest. I remember during my boyhood several examples of him putting his natural entrepreneurial talents to work. Once, he and the men of the church built a large basement addition on the church building where he was serving in central Ohio, and dad, not knowing much about the building trades, acted as the designer and general contractor on the project. Every year that same congregation operated a large food tent at the county carnival, another of dad's visions. With dad's oversight and mom's recipes, the local patrons lined up at their eatery all week long, and the resulting sales funded the youth group program for the entire year. Another of dad's legacies among long-time family friends is that somehow he found the funds to buy a church bus (his congregations were always small and underfunded). For several years dad and mom drove the youth group in that bus for a week's vacation, parents caravanning behind in those huge 1960's station wagons to the shores of the Carolinas. Many creative uses of scarce resources in dad's 40+ years of ministry brought people close to him, to his vision and his leadership. Everywhere he went, in every congregation he led, people responded to this man of stellar character and inspired guidance, especially the youth. Finally, for the last 17 years of his career dad led the chaplaincy department of a major state hospital in Indiana. Serving that population of patients was to him the pinnacle of his life's ministry, and he again gave it his utmost. I have many fond memories of his services, and ceremonies, and programs in that hospital over the course of two decades; his reaching out to the local community to build bridges between the town and the mental institution. He was inspiring to all who knew him and loved him.

My father retired at age 65. He sat down, and he turned on the TV, and didn't get up for the next 16 years. It was like someone turned off a light switch. He bought into the whole "men are supposed to retire at age 65 and stop working" myth, and it was the worst decision he ever made for himself. Coupled with that decision, he hadn't done much, if any, inner work to heal his own wounds or to affirm himself after carrying the burdens of others during decades of professional care giving. The entrepreneurial, visionary, ambitious, creative, dynamic, magnetic pastor just crashed; the emotional and spiritual wreckage lay strewn around the waysides of his soul.

My father died a broken, forlorn man. The debilitating ailment of emotional poverty, and his stubborn refusal to ultimately heal it, slowly ate away at his inner being to the extent that he died a shell of a man. The ailment broke his spirit. It was heart-wrenching to watch. There was nothing I or anybody else could do for him: it was the path he chose.

I have pondered the mystery and the sadness of my father's choices. What drove him to refuse to heal himself? How could he not feel his spirit swirling down the drain of life, and not grab hold of himself before the basin ran empty? What powers came into play in ruining this once vibrant man? How did my father wander so far from a path of health?

How often do such stories in other families play out in the same manner? The father, the husband, the grandfather distance themselves from loved ones in any number of ways because they have never taught themselves how to care for their own emotional needs. Who can be emotionally present for others when one doesn't know how to be emotionally present for oneself? These kinds of tragic situations in families, I believe, are close to reaching epidemic proportions in the culture, and our youth are carrying the fallout from them, especially the young men.

These questions emphasize the plight of many men in the American culture today. Some answers can be found in this book, for those who ask, and who seek. What I believe is needed for struggling men today, and for the culture at large, is a new set of paradigms for healthy living: a manifesto for males. I witnessed the intense inner strife that my father suffered around his emotional life as a man. I've experienced my own trials around these same issues. I see men all around me grappling with the same issues. On the maturity issue: How do I grow up all the way as a man? What does being fully mature mean? Why do I feel I have to hide my emotional self from others? Why do I believe that I can't trust other men, or that I can't relate to them in deep ways? On the virtuous living issue: What does acting nobly feel like? How do I bring a sense of virtue into my daily life? What are the actions and the principles necessary to live a virtuous life? And finally: How can I make a difference in the world? How can I bring it all together?

Unfortunately right now in our evolution as a culture, the type of training needed to provide answers to such questions is not offered in our educational system. I believe it is time for that to change. This book is intended to be part of that change. It is intended to be a handbook for living the life of a mature, noble man. It is a primer for teaching men the habits and principles necessary to lead such a life.

Our culture desperately needs its men to find themselves, to collectively wake up and once again take on the tasks that only mature men can effectively perform. Our women today are increasingly being forced to carry the burdens and play the roles traditionally and rightfully allotted to men, and they are getting fed up with it. In my view this situation is not fair, it is not right, and it needs to change. This book is for the women as much as it is for the men. Our women need support, they need a break from doing it all, and they need suitable male partners. They have no desire to coddle and tolerate little boys in grownup bodies, understandably so. It is time for men to step up. Our world needs its men. Our world needs mature men.

This book represents a method for men to step up to the plate. My mission in writing it is to help men gain their full maturity and live noble lives by presenting them with essential information they can use to clearly see themselves both as they may be right now, and as they can be — whole and complete.

An old adage comes to mind, in closing: "Chew the meat and spit out the bone." In other words, take what you need.

CHAPTER ONE

The Plight of the American Male

At the beginning of this book I shared my father's story. This story is a painfully personal matter for me, something I thought long about before I chose to include it. I have learned from mentors in life that my wounds came from my father's wounds, thus the healing of my wounds means that I must reconcile with my father, if not face to face, then inside myself, especially inside myself. These are deep currents. Countless men live their entire lives never healing from their deep father wounds. Either they have no knowledge of this dynamic operating in their lives, or they do have knowledge of it, but their fear about facing those wounds, facing down the wounding father, can be so great that the wounds get buried and remain unhealed.

Of course, deep cutting wounds of any kind always leave scars. Even more than that, unhealed wounds can fester and become infected, causing all sorts of related difficulties. It is true whether one is cut with a knife, or one is cut with psychological weaponry stemming from the father who wounds. In the case of the knife cut, if the wound is ignored or if the wound is just bandaged without being cleaned and infection sets in, then a limb could be lost, or worse. In the case of wounds from the father, if proper emotional healing is ignored or the wounds are just bandaged without a cleansing, then all kinds of debilitating, even violent, effects may surface over time. The irony is all fathers wound their sons in some way. We cannot escape this destiny as fathers and sons. This drama has been around since men have been around; it is a universal human condition.

The reality of my story was one of buried father wounds, left unhealed. For most of my adult life I had no conception of this dynamic operating in my psyche. I lived the life of an adolescent clothed in a man's body, up into my late 30's. I might largely be there still had not the inevitable traumas of life reared their ugly heads. I had no idea that my father's lifelong issues with his lack of maturity and with emotional dependency on his wife (my mother) was in fact fueling my internal demons around these same things, keeping me in a wounded state.

I did have for many years a gnawing vague impression deep inside that things weren't quite right with me. But I certainly had no clue that the root source of my core issues was wounding carried on from my father. Indeed, up until the time life hit me full in the face in my late 30's I had little notion that I even had unresolved issues. In order for healing to occur, one must first be aware that there is a wound present. The worst kind of wound is the one that lies undetected. That is the kind of wound I had.

As a result, over the course of some two decades, I did a lot of damage to myself and to my loved ones. My marriage, to a woman I loved with all my heart, slowly turned toxic (for many reasons on both sides).

For my part in it, I unintentionally ruined my closest relationship because I didn't have the maturity to handle a full-grown woman, and because I had absolutely no connection to my inner emotional life. After 20 years of it, my wife had had enough and she left me. Looking back on it, I don't blame her. We were both miserable, and she was the one who called it for what it was. That took a lot of courage.

During those years I self-medicated (burying my wounds) with recreational drugs and with alcohol, coming close to full-blown addiction more than once. The toxic marriage and the chemical dependencies meant regular tension and battling in the household, at times resulting in violent outbursts of temper with screaming and broken furniture. Of course, our children witnessed their share of our problems and were wounded themselves. Other than the loss of my marriage, my biggest regret from those times is that my actions left scars on my children, in many of the same ways that my father had left scars on me.

My story is a common one in today's world. The real tragedy I see in this story is that the outcome — divorce — could have been avoided. All of our family grew from the lessons taken from that loss: I grew, my former wife grew, and our children grew. That was the good thing. The bad thing was that a good family was ripped to shreds through the dysfunctional and ignorant actions of the grownups, and that didn't need to happen. For my part, as unbelievable as it may seem, I had very poor awareness of how toxic my marriage had become, and how instrumental a role I played in that toxicity.

Somehow I had developed the perspective over

the years that marriage is practically a battleground: spouses fight, issues are always present, tensions and resentment are a natural part of daily life, and sometimes furniture gets thrown around. I was hopelessly naive about what healthy adult life looks like and feels like. I had no consciousness of my major issues writing the story of my marriage's demise. When the marriage finally ended, I was blindsided. The wounds drove my behavior, the wounds contained my denial, but the wounds couldn't save my marriage. No one ever taught me about the wounds.

The fact is that from my late teens into my mid-twenties I needed to be taught by the elders, by older men, how to become a mature man. I was never taught. My father didn't teach me because he wasn't mature himself. His father didn't teach him, for the same reasons. No one taught any of us. Becoming and being a fully mature man is a learned behavior. Men must be taught. If they are not taught, and they remain little boys in full-grown bodies, then stories like mine happen.

I was not taught what a mature relationship with a woman looks like and feels like. I was not taught how to access and acknowledge my most basic emotions. I was not taught how to live with conscious awareness of my speech or my mannerisms or even my thought patterns. I was not taught how to receive different or opposing perspectives from my own without reacting defensively or feeling personally slighted. I was not taught how to defend myself when important personal boundaries were trespassed by another. I was not taught how to honestly, clearly

Chapter One • The Plight of the American Male

speak my own truth.

Where were the mature elders in my life? Where were the teachers? Where was the wisdom counsel? I didn't know then that I needed them or that they existed, or that they even needed to exist. No one taught me those crucial things. Regardless, I desperately needed the teaching about the importance of growing into full maturity as a man.

I came into my 20's taking on major responsibilities. I wasn't a full grown man yet, but I was now out of my parent's home and away from their protecting influence. I was managing a new marriage, living in a new town; I was siring children and buying houses and cars and furnishings and taking on debt. All of that occurred between the ages of 18 and 26, an eight-year span, yet I had only superficial counsel from any older men in my life during those critical years. A little learning came from vicarious witnessing of family behavior in my parent's household (at least my father was present for my upbringing, if not for my learning in how to be a man) and from the occasional guidance of friends.

At no time, in no way, in no context was I given or even offered any formal training in how to handle any of these major life conditions as a mature man. My world just assumed I knew, or would somehow figure it out. Well, I didn't know. I didn't have a clue. Wounds that needed healing: not a clue. There is such a thing as emotional maturity: not a clue. The tools needed to protect myself and relate confidently from my emotional center: not a clue. I was clueless, and I was a husband, and a father, and the head of a household. Where were the teachers? Why in Heaven's name would my world allow me to assume responsibility in the adult sphere (especially marriage and the raising of children) without proper training? It made no sense. It makes no sense.

This is the plight of the American man today. The story I'm telling about myself is a story very familiar to thousands, even millions of men in our culture. I believe it resonates deeply with men. The root cause of many of our social ills lies right here.

How many families would be intact right now if instead of immature males bringing the power of their wounds to bear in family life those same families were led by mature, virtuous men? How many boys would be out of trouble and off the streets or out of the penal system if they just had mature, virtuous men guiding them through the difficult growing pains of life? How many babies would come into the world having the loving support of both parents (the main determinant in those children having a fighting chance in life) if men would take responsibility for their own sexuality in a mature, virtuous manner? How many women would gain the luxury of working only one job, or even have a choice to stay at home for a time, to raise and nurture their children if the men who sired their children did the mature, virtuous thing and became equal partners in taking responsibility for raising those children? Divorce, 7 The Plight of the American Male

physical and emotional spouse abuse, child abuse, teenage delinquency and gang activity, illegitimate childbirth, absent fathers — all of these social ills can be traced to the source problem of a culture that has forgotten how to initiate its young men into mature, virtuous adulthood.

Am I laying a lot on men? You bet I am. Our culture has no mechanism to help men hold themselves accountable for their social behavior. There is no system present that teaches men how to live mature, virtuous lives. At one time the institution of the church had great influence in controlling male social behavior. That power is now substantially diminished in the mainstream culture. Mass market entertainment media has taken the church's place as primary influencer and as a result men are floundering, mindlessly seeking answers. The church did its share of using dogma and guilt to control behavior, but at least it provided a framework of civil behavior that normal folk could understand and embrace. Now that framework is considered by many to be obsolete, so men are increasingly feeling anchorless. The endless television diversions or sports diversions provide only fleeting, superficial ointments to men's perceptions of a lack of structure, of peace, of meaning and purpose in their lives. Does that let men off the hook? Not for a minute.

I believe that deep down inside most men don't want to be let off the hook. Most men want to take responsibility, want to hold themselves accountable, want to protect and provide for their own, and want to make their lives count for something. Those traits are innate in The Male Manifesto 8 the human psyche. Men increasingly don't know how to do these things. Why? They are not being taught. Does that mean that they don't need to learn? No. That means we need to find a way to once again teach them.

The initiation of men is the key that opens the door to men finding themselves again. It is the sacred balm of health to modern male culture. Male initiation is an ancient, essential tool of societal stability. It has been lost somewhere in the last many generations of Americans, but it is now slowly resurfacing among small sub-sections of the culture. I happen to be a participant in one of those sub-sections. I am an initiated man. If the learning I have gained from my personal work as an initiated man somehow makes it into the mainstream culture, more precisely if the collective learning that all initiated men have gained does so, the changes to our society will be astounding in their positive and healing impact.

Before we turn to the topic of male initiation (the practice of the mature elders taking the boys out of the world and guiding them on a personal journey that results in the adoption of their mature manhood), we first will spend some time discussing what it can look like for boys to not experience the teaching, guidance, wisdom, and support of emotionally mature men in their world. We will now touch on the world of the emasculated male.

CHAPTER TWO

The Emasculated Male

Mothers nurture their children. Fathers discipline their children. It is that simple. It takes both equal parts to raise a healthy and whole child. Can a mother discipline? Can a father nurture? Of course they can. But generally speaking mothers are much better at nurturing than disciplining and fathers are much better at disciplining than nurturing. These traits are bred in the bone; they arise out of millions of years of human evolution. They are hard wired in us humans. I have no doubts about the truth of this.

As will be discussed later in this book, women naturally come into their emotional maturity through deep connection to the female reproductive process: the biochemical birth/death/rebirth events that occur in the menstrual cycle. I believe this dynamic also comes into play in the nurturing/maternal instinct arena for women. Mothers have a special, innate capacity to nurture their young, and it, like emotional maturity, is deeply connected to the female reproductive process. A mother is naturally programmed to nurture, even when she knows that over-nurturing behavior may be harming her child. The instinct is that deeply ingrained, and it is cemented through biology. Mothers can't help themselves; they simply must nurture their young. God bless them for this.

Fathers, on the other hand, just as in the emotional maturation process, have no biologically based equivalent for the development of their natural tendencies to discipline their children. Just as with the necessity of learning emotional maturity from older mature men, so I believe it is true with learning how to effectively discipline as a father. With rare exception young men must all be taught the value and methods of disciplining from older men. Only in recent times have men begun to neglect this essential type of teaching — for most of human history discipline has been passed down through generations of men teaching men. The ingraining of this male instinct has occurred through cultural tradition rather than through biology.

Young men have a deep yearning to be disciplined by, and learn discipline from, older mature men. I think this is why the military institutions are so proficient at turning out disciplined men; men young and old resonate at their deepest levels with the value of discipline. How often have I witnessed standing in the presence of a man who has experienced the world of military discipline and felt almost a sense of awe — felt a profound strength and composure and self-discipline emanating from that man? The same holds true for me with standing in the presence of one who has experienced initiation into emotional maturity — I can almost touch and hold the quiet power emanating from that man.

Men such as these — the man with military

Chapter Two • The Emasculated Male

training and the man who has experienced initiation into maturity — are men who have been taught in profound ways by male teachers the power and strength of male discipline. This is an education that boys can't learn in a classroom, and can't be taught by women. It must be accomplished in the classroom of life, and it must be learned from other men. Only men know how to teach men the essence of male discipline.

When the teaching occurs properly, when younger, inexperienced men are taught the value and power of discipline from older, more experienced men and the transference of the knowledge is complete, then the upcoming young men are blessed with the essential tools to become the next generation of teachers, to become properly trained life companions for their women, and to become sound fathers, giving their children the gifts and blessings and tools that only sound fathers can give. In order for society as we know it to remain ordered and secure, and not deteriorate into chaos, this essential duty of men supplying discipline in the family must survive intact and be transferred from one generation to the next. It is absolutely critical to our continuation as a civilized culture.

In fact, the ancient heritage of civilized male discipline is in today's times under siege. The trends are noteworthy and alarming. We, who live in a world where the divorce rate is running north of 50% and where the judicial system is still practically antithetical to active fatherhood, often witness firsthand the scourge of no discipline through the tragedy of absent fathers in our children's lives, especially in our boys' lives.

It happens in many ways, for many reasons. Males who have reached reproductive maturity are still boys mentally and emotionally. Such men/children, when informed that they are about to become fathers, often react as boys will react by simply running away and ignoring their responsibility, regardless of who they abandon. This happens not only with teens, but with emotionally immature men in their 20's, 30's, and even 40's. The temptation to flee from a perceived major life threat supersedes any sense of personal responsibility. Such a man in such a situation will just disappear, leaving a path of emotional and material devastation behind in the fledgling family that was meant for him to guide and lead. No discipline; absent father.

At other times in other circumstances grown men will abandon their children such as when a painful, crushing divorce comes knocking at the door. Many times in our culture of divorce today the woman will be the person who ends a toxic marriage. This is often true because the woman, after years of tolerating it, is finally fed up with having to live with a man who is still emotionally an adolescent, where she feels as much or more like her husband's mother as she does his wife. In these circumstances, the immature man/boy can't emotionally handle the loss, so either he will act out by allowing spite and revenge to become primary in his interactions with his former partner, or he will retreat into a shell of emotional impotence where all his interactions with his family and with the world in general lack any sense of passion or engagement:

he assumes the mantle of defeat. In either case this man will often emotionally or physically abandon his children, the product of the union of himself and his former spouse. The pain of loss is too great to bear, so he disappears from his children's lives, or he becomes a powerless bystander.

There are other reasons than these why kids don't have their fathers in their lives. The father has died; the father is incarcerated or institutionalized; the father suffers from full-blown substance abuse and has removed himself from the family; the father also had been abandoned by his father and is simply repeating the family cycle. The reasons don't matter all that much. To me the root cause of the epidemic of absent fathers in our culture is the disconnection of men from the special heritage of discipline.

What happens to boys who don't have fathers in their lives, and by "father" I mean one or more older men who embody the fathering energy? They either grow up to be feral — violent destroyers of the culture — or they grow up to be emasculated, or both. Who raises boys without fathers present? Most often the mothers do. Sometimes it is the grandmothers who do; sometimes it is other extended family members, and sometimes it is the foster home. In any case when the father is absent the mother energy has no complementary father energy as a balancing presence in the child's life. The mother energy will kick in well beyond what is healthy; the male child will often rebel against what he feels as smothering, and rightfully so. Boys have a natural repugnance to being smothered. Mother now has to wear two hats — those of nurturer and disciplinarian. She does her best to be both kinds of emotional provider for her child, which is of course impossible, at least at optimal levels. This is not how God intended family life to be conducted, so naturally all manner of problems ensue.

Mothers are not likely to enforce their wills on their boys beyond a certain point and will back off disciplining them in even the smallest incidents when what the boy needs most at the moment is precisely the opposite. This is natural and should not be seen as weak or inappropriate behavior by a mother because mothers nurture, and that is all that should reasonably be asked of them. A little vignette will illustrate the point: Mother gives Billy a bowl of cereal for breakfast before school. Billy looks at the cereal and announces he wants a waffle instead. Mom tells him to eat his cereal — he is not getting a waffle; she is not going to waste a good bowl of cereal. Billy either just sits there and stares at the cereal or pouts and whines to mom. Mom caves in to Billy's manipulation; she removes the bowl from in front of him and makes him a waffle all the while consoling him, or complaining out loud about his behavior, or both. Billy gets his way and learns just a little bit more about how to manipulate mom into getting what he wants.

If a sound father were present in this scene, he would see early on in the exchange what was happening and would step in to support mom, telling Billy firmly to "get it going" and eat his cereal. There would be no pouting and whining; there would be no further attempts at manipulation, and most importantly there would be no waffle

Chapter Two • The Emasculated Male

appearing. Billy would go to school hungry, if necessary, and he would then have an opportunity to learn that he'd better mind his parents or there would be consequences. Dad's natural sense of discipline helps Billy to learn healthy masculine behavior, and mom doesn't have to do something that is against her nature. This is how it is supposed to work.

The vignette of Billy and the cereal can be amplified into larger life circumstances. The story of a boy growing up in today's world with no father present might be told something like this.

Joey sat with his arms wrapped around knees drawn up into his chest on the curb at the end of his street and watched the traffic roll by. He felt relieved to be away from that house, again. Seemed like this curb had become his second home. He could sit here, nobody to bother him — the motion of the cars easing his nerves and the sounds of the traffic drowning out his thoughts. He hated his mom — hated her. She had done it again — didn't matter to her how he felt about it. She said she cared about his feelings, but she went on and did it again anyway.

It was just like the last time. The man had been nice enough to begin with, had even brought Joey a baseball mitt and ball and played catch with him. But then, after a while Joey's mom started doing the same things just like she had done with so many men before this one. Joey's mom started letting this man dominate her; she wouldn't stick up for herself. It would get worse and worse until Joey couldn't stand it anymore, and he would explode at the man in his mom's presence. It would always end up being an ugly scene, every time, and Joey would always end up bolting from the house to get away. Joey had no respect for his mom, hated that she put him through this over and over, hated all the men that came around, hated himself — hated his life.

Joey's mom always tried to make it up to him after these scenes. She would let him get away with almost anything. When Joey yelled and screamed at her, she would try to control him, but he knew she would just end up giving in to him. She bought him all kinds of things he didn't need — clothes and games and cell phones —and he would break them just so she would have to buy him more. She didn't make him do his homework, didn't make him go to bed at a decent hour, didn't really set any boundaries around when he came and went. Joey knew his mom loved him, but he saw that she felt really weak with him; that she felt guilty Joey had the life he did. Joey wished his mom would figure out how to be strong with him. She worked hard at her job as a hotel manager, and she made enough money to pay their bills and have some nice things too. Things were not what Joey wanted. His mom could not buy his respect.

Joey could feel there was something very wrong in his house, and with himself, but he didn't know what it was, and his mom sure didn't have the answers. The more she tried showing Joey her love and consoling him and protecting him, the more resentful he became toward her. He felt a deep emptiness — a longing for something that he couldn't identify but that was missing in his life. Joey had a good roof over his head, plenty of food to eat, all the possessions a teenage boy could want, and a mom who doted over him and loved him. But Joey felt utterly lost and alone.

Joey had been in his father's presence twice in his life. The first time was at Joey's grandmother's funeral when he was a little boy. Joey remembered his dad had on a dark suit and black shoes, and he remembered his dad saying hello to him and asking him how he was doing, but his dad had not touched Joey in any way. Joey wanted to touch his dad, to hug him. That never happened. The second time his father came to take Joey out for a milk shake and a talk. They had sat in a booth in the ice cream shop while they ate, and his dad did most of the talking. He told Joey that he loved him and thought about him a lot; that he was a bad father, but he just couldn't handle the responsibility of raising a child; that Joey's mom had gotten pregnant by accident and that he was never meant to be a father. Joey mostly listened and said very little. He felt the whole time like he just wanted his dad to reach out and embrace and hold him — it hurt so much. His dad shook Joey's hand at the end of their visit and told Joey he would come get him again soon to go out together and do something. He never came.

Joey withdrew more and more into his shell, away from the world. None of the adults in his life understood him — mom didn't, teachers didn't, counselors didn't. Joey found solace in the streets. At least the people who hung out in the streets understood the anger he felt. Everyone who hung out in the streets was angry. They used common street tools to express their anger: fights, guns, drugs, alcohol, sex, betrayal, abuse. Joey learned these ways. His mother was powerless to stop him and could only watch with mounting fear that Joey would get hurt, or worse. She especially abhorred the way her son treated women. Joey had a knack of finding girls who were needy and weak, and he would abuse them, not physically, but emotionally: not committing to a relationship in any way, demeaning them in public, and cheating on them. It was horrible; he was horrible. He had no male friends to speak of; said he didn't trust men. He felt that men had betrayed him, abandoned him.

And then it happened. Late one Saturday night Joey came home with his latest girl and found his mom on the couch with another man who he'd never seen before. Joey had been drinking heavily, and when he saw his mom in the arms of that man, Joey cracked. He ended up in jail after the police wrestled him to the ground in his mom's front yard, not for accosting his mom or the strange man but for beating up the girl who was with him at the time. Joey had lost it and had physically injured another. All the anger and feelings of abandonment and betrayal had boiled over, and the consequences of his actions had now landed him in the system, with a criminal record. Joey faced a long road back to normal life, if that was even possible. He was dealt a bad hand, which he had played badly, with no guidance from the people who could give him what he needed, no guidance from older, wise, mature, strong men.

∽

Chapter Two • The Emasculated Male 21

Sam's was another story altogether. He grew up at the other end of the emasculated male spectrum.

Sam had a father just like Joey did, but unlike Joey, Sam's father was in Sam's life. Sam lived in the suburbs in a big, beautiful house with a swimming pool and a three- car garage and five acres of land. Sam's mother was able to stay at home and raise her kids full time because Sam's father made a lot of money. Sam had two sisters, one younger and one older than he. Sam was with his mother and his sisters all the time. He got to see his father, Brad, for an hour or two in the evenings and sometimes on Sunday afternoons.

Sam was a happy boy; he had been sheltered from the ugliness of the world. His mom was always there for him, he got along well with his sisters, and even though dad seemed to be working all the time and Sam had no real connection with him, at least Sam knew his father was there: they lived in the same house together.

The father, Brad, had his own practice as a civil engineer. Brad's routine was to be up and in the office by 7AM every morning, six days a week, to be home by 8PM for dinner, and to see the kids for an hour before their bedtime. Sunday was "family day," when the wife and kids were to join Brad for non-work-related activities. It was a very ordered life for Brad. He felt he was doing the best for his family by being a good provider and devoting all of his energies to growing his business.

The home, in Brad's mind, was his wife's domain. It was her responsibility to make sure their daily needs were met — all their needs. In Brad's mind there was a proper and distinct division of parental duties, so that was the way Brad's household ran. Brad brought home the bacon, and his wife raised the children, tended the marriage, and ensured domestic tranquility.

Brad was emotionally unavailable to anyone in his life, including his family. Brad allowed himself no access to his feelings. Whenever emotions came close to the surface, except for anger, Brad had learned the tactics to shut them off — to bury them. In Brad's mind everything in life could be reasoned out in an orderly manner. There was no need for emotional displays, or for feelings in general. He had learned this from his father.

Brad's father, Ernest, was a leader in the community, a manufacturing agent, a functional alcoholic, and an emotional tyrant toward his wife and children, toward Brad. Ernest's father had died when Ernest was a boy, so Ernest was raised by the women in his life, his mother and his aunts. The outcome of this upbringing created a toxic stew in Ernest — a recipe of resentment, of emotional distance from others and emotional dependence on women. Ernest did not gain the benefits of growing up being guided and taught by older men in his life — no father, grandfather, or uncles present. He learned about life in his boyhood from women. Since the essential male guidance boys must receive in order to mature into men was denied him, Ernest came to resent the feminine-based influences he did receive: nurturing, emotional expression, depth of relationships, honest communication, and so on. At the same time, from his youngest days on, Ernest looked to women out of necessity as authority figures. Thus, he developed the unhealthy habit of always deferring to women on matters of importance, and looking for their leadership and guidance during conflict or life crisis.

The unhealthy paradox for Ernest was that he resented women because they had failed to provide for him at his deepest levels as a male, yet he felt dependent on women. If a woman became upset with him, even as an adult, Ernest's inner wounded little boy would surface, and that little boy would always respond outwardly with petulance, defensiveness, and immature pride. Ernest went to his grave an unhealed and deeply tormented man. He passed that legacy on to his son, Brad, who in turn passed it on to his son, Sam.

Brad, the son, learned from his father and carried his father's wounds, just as all boys learn from their fathers and carry their father's wounds. Brad had little direct knowledge of his own wounding coming from his father's wounds, but he sensed somehow that he carried a tragic legacy. He had witnessed firsthand how his father frequently insulted and demeaned his mother. He had learned that fathers were distant and cold authority figures, not to be disrespected, and people to whom no vulnerability or weakness was ever shown.

In many ways Brad did not want the same toxicity and unhappiness from his childhood to consume his own family, his wife and children. Brad consciously attempted to be present for them. He made time for family interactions at dinner and on Sundays. He made an effort to show up for school functions, and for birthdays, and occasionally for a doctor's appointment. But Brad unconsciously carried the wounding from his father into his own family dynamic. He interacted with his children primarily at a superficial level; deeper connections were foreign to him. He carried his responsibility as the family disciplinarian seriously, yet he did not want to be confronted with any potentially hurtful issues in the lives of family members. When his wife or children approached him with uncomfortable issues, Brad would clam up, either giving them a dismissive answer or brushing the issue off by telling them they would talk about it "later" and then ignoring the issue altogether. He treated his wife with a combination of disdain and adoration. It happened regularly that one minute Brad would insult his wife in front of the children and in the next minute sing her praises as an excellent mother or an excellent cook. The children could tell intuitively that their father both loved and hated his wife. They witnessed continually that whenever their mother either attempted to express her true feelings to Brad or challenge him in any way, he would first become brutish and overbearing and then subside into moody, immature complacency. The powerful, confident civil engineer turned into a wounded, lost husband and father at home. Brad unconsciously brought the wounding from his father, Ernest, into his own family dynamic. Something deep inside Brad prevented him from facing the wounds his father passed on to him, and Brad's family paid the price, especially his son, Sam.

And so we come to Sam, Brad's son, Ernest's

Chapter Two • The Emasculated Male 25

grandson. Sam is a gifted boy, intelligent like his father and sweet of spirit like his mother. He is the apple of his mother's eye, and she is the center of his universe. Sam is the middle child of the three children. He is introverted, a reader and a thinker, not into the traditional male pursuits like sports, cars, and the outdoors. Sam stays around the house most of the time, helping with the chores and playing with his sisters. He has a couple of uncles who don't come around very much, and one living grandfather who he sees a few times a year. Sam's mother stays at home most of the time too, taking care of the household and sometimes having women friends visit to sit and chat over a cup of tea. Sam's sisters do the typical sister thing, spatting about time in the bathroom before school and commiserating about the latest boy interests, and other sisterly topics. Sam's father works all the time, occasionally being seen sitting at the kitchen table on a Sunday morning with a cup of coffee and the newspaper in hand, and also occasionally talking with Sam about a report card or mowing the grass.

Sam has few friends; the ones he does have are female. Sam doesn't like being with boys all that much; they are strange to him and he doesn't trust them. He certainly can't talk with them like he can with his female friends. Sam is attracted to females; the way they look and their scent stir deep waters in him. But he is frightened by them: he doesn't understand their power over him and their mysterious ways. He shies away from the ones who stir those deep waters in him. He tries hard to please the other females, all of them: his mother, his sisters, his female friends. Females surround Sam's life, and he feels comforted, protected — nurtured.

Sam has never experienced danger in his life. He has never had to find his own food, fend for himself in any way; never had to contemplate his own survival. It has all been given to him. His mother has always been there for him, to comfort him when he's upset, to give him what he needs to remain content. Even though he can't talk with his father about anything going on inside himself, and can't talk with other boys, he can talk with his mother; she always understands and always takes away the pain. When his mother or his sisters become upset about anything, regardless the reason, Sam takes it personally and will become openly angry and defensive with them, cutting off any opportunity for mutual discussion. He can't tolerate witnessing them becoming upset, even when their emotional displays have nothing to do with him. At the same time, Sam will do his best to appease them, giving in to their emotional outbursts. Sam does the same with other people out in the world, absorbing slights and insults, not standing up for himself, and generally letting himself be trod upon while keeping a grin on his face and burying his hurt.

Sam is powerless with the females in his life; he has little conception of the world of males, and the little he does perceive he doesn't understand and doesn't trust. Because of his raising and the female-centered household in his youth, and because of the father wounding passed to him through several generations, Sam has few tools at his disposal to help him grow into healthy mature adult masculinity.

Chapter Two • The Emasculated Male

Sam's path, unless something dramatic intervenes to correct the course, will lead him to a life devoid of emotional connection, to an unhealthy dependence on women, and to the avoidance and distrust of any relationships with male friends or mentors, thus setting him up to stay stuck as an emotional adolescent all of his days. Sam will never be at peace unless he frees himself from such a self-imposed prison.

Both Joey and Sam are products of absent fathers, one whose father was physically absent and one whose father was emotionally absent. Both boys were raised primarily by their mothers. One boy chose the path of violence and social disruption, and the other boy chose a less visible but just as damaging path of passivity and emotional dependency. Both boys live in a continual state of naivete, in other words a fundamental ignorance of what it means to be a full-grown mature man. An overabundance of feminine energy in their lives and a tragic absence of positive masculine energy tell the tale for both boys. These boys will carry their unhealed father wounds into adult relationships and into interactions with, and conceptions of, the larger world. That world will suffer as a result.

In the next section, we jump away from the modern, civilized world to a time and a place different from what we know and what we're used to. The time might be, from our modern perspective, long ago. The place might be, from our modern perspective, primitive and archaic. The topic to be covered is male initiation. It is a topic foreign and unsettling to many of us living now, in these times. It is a topic critical to the health of young men, and thus to our culture as a whole. It is a shocking and dangerous topic. And it is a topic that can bring unheard of advancement to human life as we know it.

CHAPTER THREE

Male Initiation in Other Cultures

For the purposes of this book, I will present a simplified overview of the topic of male initiation. There is some substantive coverage of male initiation in scholarly and popular literature although not nearly enough to do justice to such a critically important facet of civilized culture. For in-depth study I would direct the reader to authors such as Margaret Mead, Robert Bly, Robert Moore, Malidoma Somé, and Michael Meade.

Initiation rituals and rites of passage abound in cultures around the world, from times before the written word up through today. Initiation represents a portal from one sphere of living into another, from the state of unknowing to the state of knowing, from youth to adulthood, from naivete to wisdom, from the outer world to the secret inner sanctum. Countless groups in countless contexts throughout history have used initiation to unify their causes and set their constituents apart from others. Some examples would be the Knights Templar, monks of various religious orders such as the Catholic Franciscans or the Tibetan Buddhists, branches of the military such as the Marines or the Cavalry, and the various Greek life organizations on college campuses. Beyond specialty groups such as these, entire cultures have used the socialization tool of male initiation to structure large portions of daily communal life. A story like the one I'm about to tell might occur amongst the aborigines of Australia, or the highlanders of New Guinea, or the native inhabitants of the Amazon river basin. The story sounds like this.

Oro sat scrunched up on the mud floor of the thatched hut, knees drawn up to his chest. It was so dark the boy couldn't see his hand in front of his face. Oro was cold, so cold he couldn't stop shivering. The hunger didn't feel as overpowering as the day before; this morning he and the other boys had been given some fruit to eat. The sounds of the night jungle were both soothing and frightening. Oro was not accustomed to being away from his mother and his village like this; it was all so new and strange. Oro felt in his bones that the shivering was not just from the cold. Oro was terrified; he just wanted to go home.

The journey away from the village had happened suddenly, without warning. The journey took Oro out of his life at home, and he was not prepared. Oro was happy with his life in the village. He played with the other children every day, some of them much younger than he. He often ran with the other boys to the perimeters of the village, sometimes chasing one of the pigs, sometimes hiding in the taro fields, sometimes fighting each other with sticks, boys his own age.

Life in the village was not easy. Often there was not enough food, and often his father and the other men were gone for long periods, leaving the women and the old people to care for things. But the village seemed safe to Oro; it was always there for him. More importantly Oro's mother was always there for him. When he hurt himself while playing, he would run to his mother and she would comfort him. When the sounds of the night scared him, his mother was there to soothe his fears. She was his safety. He didn't even think about it. Mother was always there; the village was always there. This was Oro's world.

Then one day it all changed. Oro was busy running with his friends out in the forest close to the village when they heard the drum. That sound of the drum made them stop in their tracks. They had heard that sound only once or twice ever before. Oro and his friends gazed blankly at each other, wondering what to do. They had all been told many times, "remember the drum." Just the day before, Oro's mother had told him again (it seemed for the hundredth time), "remember the drum." When she said it that time, it sounded different; her voice had a tone of mystery about it, like she knew something was going to happen. Suddenly one of the boys shouted, "Let's go!" and they all took off at a great pace back toward the village.

When the boys arrived they found the men of the village gathered together in the village center, standing and facing them. This was strange, thought Oro. Just the night before the men had left for a new adventure away, and when they did that, they were always gone for a long time. Oro saw his mother standing with the other women at the periphery away from the men, and he ran to her, feeling something was about to happen. He embraced his mother and she turned him around to face the gathered men, holding him close to her. That's when the danger of the moment dawned on Oro. As he witnessed the looks in the men's eyes directed at him and the other boys, he could feel it in his bones: they were coming back for him and things would never be the same, ever again.

His mother screamed as two of the men tore Oro from her embrace, just as the other mothers had each screamed when the same thing happened to their boys. When Oro's mother screamed, the two men holding the boy told her in their native tongue, "Be still; let him go." All the other mothers heard the same admonishment: "Be still; let him go." The mothers screamed in return: "Oh my baby, my boy — you will kill him!" And they wailed, each one of them.

∼

Oro sat cross legged on the mud floor of the thatched hut, and he remembered. Things were different now — things he could name, and things he couldn't name. They were all different. The world had changed, and he had changed. Mostly, he had changed — inside.

Oro remembered the journey. It began with his sense of doom at being ripped bodily from his hysterical mother's arms. Once Oro realized that his struggles were useless against the men who pulled him away, he resigned himself to capture and let the men lead him to the gathering spot, where the men had brought the other boys.

The men in the village wasted no time when they had the boys gathered together. In single file, with the village leaders in front, the men led the boys out of the main entry from the village, along a path disappearing soon into the deep forest. The men and boys traveled this path for hours, stopping at a well-used camp at sundown to build fire, eat of their stores, and rest for the night. Other than giving them food and water, the men ignored the boys completely.

The next day it was the same, and the day after that. On the third day the trek into the jungle ceased and the ordeal began. For many days thereafter Oro and his fellow boy-mates fought for their very survival, tasted death, and found themselves at the end transformed. Most of the boys made it through; one boy did not. The ordeal involved abandonment in the jungle: it meant no food or water outside of what each boy could find using his natural abilities; it meant exposure to attacks from wild beasts; it meant terrifying visits late at night from ghosts and skeletons that pierced and scarred the boys' flesh so severely that they would bear those wounds for life. After days of torturous survival Oro's natural defenses felt on the verge of collapse. He was exhausted — physically, emotionally, and spiritually.

Not wanting to succumb to the overwhelming power of the jungle, yet strangely not wanting to return to the comfort of the village and his mother's arms either, Oro waited. Sitting in the darkened hut with the other boys, all of them positioned in a circle around the perimeter walls scrunched up with knees drawn into their chests on the damp, cold earthen floor, Oro and the boys waited for the next trial. They had been locked in the hut several hours; moonlight began to shine through the cracks of the thatched roof, and the boys could just make out one another. The rest time felt welcome to all present, after seemingly endless days of hell. As Oro crouched and waited, alone in his silence in the room with the other boys, he could begin to feel vaguely the changes that had taken place inside him. It felt in his body like something deep had died, that some deep part of him had been attacked, and conquered, and killed. From this death sense Oro felt empty and alone and vulnerable; he felt that the tiniest ant could overwhelm him. Yet another part of him felt mighty and strong and at peace; he felt the thrill of facing a lethal foe and coming out the victor. Looking around the room he could see in the other boys' eyes that they were feeling the same things. The room was silent. None of the boys were crying anymore, none of them were curled up on the floor anymore. A sense of anticipation was thick in the air.

The door of the thatched hut suddenly swung open, moonlight flooded the room momentarily blinding the boys, and although they couldn't see clearly, they could hear and feel a couple of the men standing over them in the center of their crouching circle. As their vision returned, they made out two of the village warriors, attired in full warrior regalia, eying them sternly. One of the warriors commanded the boys to stand and follow him single-file out of the hut. As the boys got in line and followed the lead escort, the second escort fell in behind the line and began screaming the village war chant at full volume.

By now the boys were used to such outbursts; they had heard that screaming war chant time and time again over the last many days. As they emerged one by one from the hut, each of the boys in turn saw before him a sight he would keep in memory the rest of his life. Dozens of men, all dressed in war regalia, stood before the boys, all of them assembled around an enormous blazing bonfire. There were many more men present than those who had left the village with the boys, and it was obvious that all men there had arrived to witness this important event, whatever it was.

The boys emptied out of the hut flanked by the two warriors sent to fetch them. They were then positioned to fill an empty place kept open for them in the circle of warriors around the bonfire. As the boys faced the roaring fire and the powerful men that encircled it, one of the warrior leaders raised his clenched fists, stretched his arms fully over his head, and violently shook a war spear up and down. Throwing back his head, he let go with a tremendous guttural scream into the night jungle air. Following his lead all the other warriors present did the same. The collective voice of the men was deafening.

The boys remained silent and did not flinch at the immense display of male energy. They all felt a mixture of terror and elation. None of them could deny the thrill of connection to that primal male sound, which stirred them profoundly. Somehow they all knew: that sound represented the change that had transformed each one of them. Something new had been born inside, and something that was supposed to die had died inside. And it felt right.

The leader ceased his wild cry and lowered his arms, and the other men followed suit. Another man left his station, circled the fire toward the group of waiting boys and stopped to face the boy on the farthest left of their line. The man stared hard, up close into the boy's eyes, and then instructed the boy in a low, even tone to follow him. The man and the boy circled the fire and stopped in front of the leader, facing him. The boy's guide then stepped away.

As the entire group watched in silence, the leader got nose to nose with the boy, spoke in a volume that only he and the boy could hear for a time, then took a spear handed to him from a man standing close by, placed the shaft of the spear on its side in each of the boy's hands, grasped each of the boy's wrists with his two hands, yanked the boy's arms holding the spear over the boy's head and repeated his wild cry, echoed by all the other men in the group. The boy returned to his position in the circle holding his newly earned warrior's spear, and the guide collected the next boy for presentation to the leader. Each of the boys in turn was presented to the leader and received his words, his spear, and a raging war cry. The ritual repeated itself until all boys had made their trip to the leader.

When Oro's turn came to stand before the leader, he did so and was immediately drawn in, mesmerized by the warrior's penetrating stare. Unable to move or tear his eyes away from that commanding gaze digging into his soul, Oro heard these words spoken in a voice that was meant for him only:

"Boy, look at me. From this moment on, let no two-legged ever again call you boy. You have made the journey. You have died and now you live anew. You have overcome. Now, Oro, let all men call you man!"

Then, in full-throated volume, the leader threw up Oro's arms and screamed into his face:

"YOU—ARE—WARRIOR!!!"

∽

At the edge of the taro fields children were chasing mice. Hearing the first sound, they raised their heads, on the alert for strangers. When the procession of men entered the clearing from the jungle and the children recognized them, they ran squealing back to the village. As the men entered the village center single-file, each carrying upright his spear, the children jumped up and down around them yelping their cheers of welcome, while the women again stood at the periphery, this time aloof and seemingly uninterested in the men's return.

Oro approached his mother, who stood straight-backed and proud in front of him. Oro looked deeply into her eyes for a time, and then gently put his arms around her for a time. When he had finished, he kissed her on the cheek, looked again deeply into her eyes and turned to rejoin the men. As he walked away, Oro's mother took a deep breath and let it slowly out, a half-smile appearing on her lips and a knowing gaze focusing her eyes. Oro's mother had seen what she was hoping to see: the men had done their job, and Oro had done his. Her little boy was dead and gone. There was now a new man in her life. Her job was done, and she could rest.

∼

This tale of male initiation in primitive cultures speaks to a forgotten tradition, that of older mature men taking their boys out of the world of daily life and guiding them through a necessary, ritual process of initiation into manhood. Using the tool of a severe life trial, the men help the boy kill his naivete, his innocent helpless little boy, and adopt his human divine birthright: the life of an engaged, mature man. This is known as the hero's journey, and it is essential to the life of a healthy, mature human male. Advancing civilization, prosperity, technology, and life beyond interdependence with the earth have caused our culture to slowly forget this essential tradition.

What did Oro go on to do in life? He embraced his village as a man, and gained clarity about his necessary role in keeping it functioning and healthy. He took his learning from the initiation and put it to work. He learned to see himself as a provider and protector rather than as a dependent and a user. He learned to give rather than to take. He learned that his word is his bond. He learned that wisdom comes from within, and it is essential to healthy community, and it takes much practice to use it adeptly. He learned how to be a mature man.

Chapter Three • Male Initiation in Other Cultures 41

∽

The next chapter covers the topic of living a virtuous life. In our quest to identify the qualities necessary to be a fully alive, healthy, authentic, mature, noble man, we must go beyond the realm of male initiation and maturity, into the realm of virtue. Let's go there now.

∾ CHAPTER FOUR ∾
Living a Virtuous Life

In the lives of humans the practice of virtue contains both external and internal dynamics. Externally, virtue has to do with modes of behavior or codes of conduct. has to do with modes of behavior or codes of conduct. Honesty is an external act of virtue that involves the behavior of truth-telling; it is directed outward toward the world. The same is true of other external acts of virtue such as bravery, perseverance, and empathy.

Inwardly, virtue is a state of being, that of living a virtuous life. Living in this state of being begins with something called personal integrity, which is at the very core of inner virtue. Indeed, there is a direct correlation between the depth of personal integrity and the depth of living a virtuous life. This is true because the attribute of personal integrity and the state of being of inner virtue are both connected to God consciousness. In this connection they proportionally relate to one another.

What is this quality called personal integrity? Simply put, it is the practice of consciously following one's own personal set of principles; one's code of ethics; one's moral compass. Personal integrity actually is comprised of two separate yet connected facets: first, knowledge of and clarity about exactly what one's principles of right living are; and second, the willingness to uncompromisingly adhere to those principles. The greater the knowledge and clarity, and the stronger the adherence, the deeper the personal integrity. Once a man's particular knowledge, clarity, and adherence to his principles are learned and practiced, that man intuitively knows when he is "in" integrity with himself (and thus with the outside world) at any given time, and when he is "out of " integrity with himself. The more a man consciously chooses through his daily actions to be "in" integrity with himself (and thus with the outside world) by uncompromisingly living by his principles, the more that man will express virtuous behavior.

Let's illustrate this dynamic with an example. Suppose a principle of living I find to be of great importance and that I adhere to is: showing respect for my elders at all times. If I am "in" personal integrity with this principle, I will display one set of behaviors. If I am "out of " personal integrity with this principle, I will display another set of behaviors. Being "in" integrity I may take actions such as addressing an elder as "Sir" or "Ma'am" or by their last name rather than their first name, assisting an elder to get out of a vehicle or into a building, deferring to an elder's wisdom about a matter without argument on my part, or allowing an elder to go ahead of me in line rather than behind me. Being "out of " integrity I may take actions such as thinking about my elders, or actually calling my elders, old and worn out, interrupting an elder when he is trying to make a point and is taking his time in doing so, or verbally attacking an elder out of frustration with having to deal with his frailties.

In the first instance being "in" integrity with the principle of showing respect for my elders at all times means that a) I know that this is an important principle of right living for me, and I have clarity about what that looks like in my actions, and b) I am willing to adhere to that principle by not compromising on consistent, respectful behavior at all times toward my elders. This being "in" integrity inner state with its consequent outward behaviors brings me the rewards of self-affirmation, peace and serenity, and acknowledgement that I am directly contributing to good in the world.

Conversely, in the second instance being "out of " integrity with the principle of showing respect for my elders at all times means that a) I know that this is an important principle of right living for me but I don't have clarity about what that looks like in my actions, or b) I do not know about the importance of this principle in my life so I don't have either the knowledge or the clarity, or c) I have knowledge and I have clarity but my willingness to adhere to this principle is low or even nonexistent so my actions are incongruent with the knowledge and the clarity, and I am at risk to do the opposite of treating my elders with respect at all times: disrespect them. The being "out of " integrity inner state with its consequent outward behaviors will often bring me troubles — feelings of shame and guilt, anger at myself and at the world, and maybe even increasingly disrespectful behavior toward my elders. Thus, living a virtuous life, and expressing virtuous behaviors, is directly relational to personal integrity, the quality of knowing, having clarity about, and firmly adhering to a personal code of ethics. Certainly, a man can perform isolated acts of virtuous behavior outside of being "in" integrity with himself. But I do not believe a man can possess personal integrity and not live a virtuous life. Hence, personal integrity is foundational to living a virtuous life.

Another essential quality follows personal integrity in forming the inner conditions for living a virtuous life. Closely linked with clarity around one's personal code of ethics, this quality has to do with conscious awareness: it is the attribute of mindfulness.

Life amongst humans abounds with everyday opportunities to practice virtuous behavior. As is true with all aspects of life, not only do the major events determine the depth and value of one's journey on this planet, so do the thousands of seemingly inconsequential events. Mindfulness, the state of conscious awareness, is what allows a man to derive meaning from life's minute details. Mindfulness assists a man in taking advantage of everyday opportunities to practice virtuous living. It is mindfulness that prevents a man from blindly missing those everyday opportunities.

Let's return to the example of showing respect for one's elders at all times in order to illustrate these points about mindfulness. Suppose for a moment that I am a fast-running businessman. I have just left my home first thing in the morning and am driving my usual route to the office. From experience I know

Chapter Four • Living a Virtuous Life

that it takes 13 minutes to get from my driveway to the office parking lot in normal traffic. I must be at the office at 8AM to receive an important client. I back out of my driveway at 7:40, which will give me precisely seven minutes to get from the car to my office at work once I arrive. As is my habit, I leave little margin for error in making that timeframe work.

Everything is going as planned on the drive in, up until the time I come upon a car in front of me cruising along at 10 mph under the speed limit (and almost 20 mph under my speed). The road is two-lane with a no-passing zone all the way along my route, the driver of the car ahead shows every indication that she will continue at this speed, and I realize quickly that I am stuck behind her. I also notice from seeing the white hair in the driver's seat ahead that I have come upon an elder woman, bad news for my plans.

Assessing this dilemma, I am now faced with a set of choices. One choice is to do everything in my power to speed up the elder's driving, or to somehow navigate my way around her. Some behaviors around that choice could be: drive right up to her rear bumper, tailgating her car, to give her a clear message to speed up; honk my horn multiple times to give her that message; roll my window down and yell and gesture to her; attempt to pass her in the no-passing zone with traffic coming the other way. All of these behaviors would be disrespectful toward the elder woman. All of these behaviors would cause my stress level to rise, thus putting me in a bad frame of mind for my meeting with the client. All of these behaviors would cause me to be "out of " integrity with myself regarding the principle in my personal code of ethics to show respect to my elders at all times.

Another set of choices altogether is to take this everyday opportunity to practice virtuous living by using the quality of mindfulness. Using mindfulness, I am able to assess the situation in this manner: I have followed my normal routine in my normal timeframe to make an important meeting with a client; if this elderly lady doesn't soon turn off the road, her slow driving will cause me to be late. But, truth be told, whose fault is this, really? Just because I am hurrying doesn't mean that she should be too. Her life is completely removed from mine, and she has no idea that I have put myself on a tight timeframe. She might be driving slowly because she knows her driving reflexes are slower, and she wants to be careful. She might be driving slowly because her eyesight is bad. It doesn't actually matter because my little dilemma is not hers. I should not be imposing on her just because I didn't give myself enough margin-for-error in making my meeting on time. I should have left my house at 7:30, instead of 7:40, and then none of this would be an issue. This is my own fault, not hers.

Now, once such an assessment is made an entirely different set of actions can take place. Some behaviors might be: take a deep breath or two and ease my foot off the accelerator; say a reassuring word to myself about not panicking; put myself in this woman's shoes about what she might be facing in her life; remind myself that it is better to apologize for being late than to endanger myself and someone else because of unsafe driving. All of these behaviors show respect for the elderly woman. All of these behaviors would allow me to be "in" integrity with myself around the principle in my personal code to show respect to my elders at all times. By using the quality of mindfulness to see the larger picture in this everyday incident, I have taken advantage of an opportunity to practice virtuous living. I have exhibited the virtuous behaviors of patience, kindness, fortitude, and respect for another.

This example shows how one can use mindfulness in combination with personal integrity to engage in virtuous living, especially during tense or alarming circumstances when it would be easy to behave selfishly or inappropriately.

Finally, a third essential quality is needed along with personal integrity and mindfulness in forming the ideal inner conditions for living a virtuous life. This is the quality called charity, in its original and truest sense.

Today, charity is viewed simplistically as giving aid to the poor. Yet there is a much deeper meaning to the term, and it has to do with love. This deeper notion of charity marches in close step with the faith perspective that all of creation is an extension of God; that all humans come from God and belong to God. Charity steeped in such a faith perspective is the outward manifestation of one's love of God, love of oneself, and finally love of, and benevolence toward, one's fellow humans. The key element here is love. It is the kind of love that involves giving selflessly, putting others before oneself, walking in another's shoes, sacrificing so that others may prosper, and showing compassion, mercy, and forgiveness even when others don't deserve it.

Let's return one last time to the example of our man who is stuck behind the slow-driving elder woman. We'll assume that he has chosen virtuous actions regarding his dilemma. This man recognizes his personal ethic of respecting elders at all times. He chooses his actions intentionally and accordingly; thus he is "in" integrity with his own value system. He is mindful that any action he takes, however small, either supports or detracts from his personal integrity. He is mindful that this situation is an everyday opportunity to practice actions that support his personal integrity. So he chooses to subordinate his priority to be on time to meet his client to his higher priority to respect elders at all times. He chooses to slow down to match the elder's speed. He takes a few deep breaths to calm himself. He tells himself that this small inconvenience will pass soon. He intentionally looks at things other than the woman in front of him — the trees lining the road, the white clouds in the blue, sunlit sky — things that will help calm him. When she does finally turn off and the road opens again in front of him, he doesn't honk or gesture rudely or race around her aggressively; he refrains from any angry behavior. Our man lets go of the situation and resumes his drive into the office as if it never happened.

Unbeknownst to the elder woman driver, this man has just treated her in a very charitable manner. He found himself in a situation directly involving her where his needs were negatively affected by

Chapter Four • Living a Virtuous Life 51

hers. He recognized immediately that: a) he prided himself on always being respectful to elders, and b) he had limited choices in this situation. He chose to put her needs before his own; chose to not escalate a situation that would upset her and possibly even endanger her; chose to show her an act of charity and thus show his community an act of service. All the small actions our man chose to take around this situation were acts of charity.

Our example of the driver and the elder woman illustrates the three inner conditions necessary for living a virtuous life: personal integrity, mindfulness, and charity. The driver called on and put into play his personal integrity when he did not compromise on his ethic of always respecting his elders. The driver used mindfulness to control the situation by seeing the larger picture, by not acting impulsively, and by consciously calming himself in order to behave in a virtuous manner. The driver showed the woman consciously chosen acts of charity, or love, when he backed off, walked in her shoes, put her needs before his own, and allowed the situation to dissipate without directing any hostile behavior toward her.

We can apply this recipe for living a virtuous life in practically all contexts and at all times. It works with large life issues and with isolated daily events. It works in all interpersonal relations: with spouses, children, parents, friends, acquaintances, coworkers, and strangers. It works with situations that are here one moment and gone the next, and with situations that develop over many years. It is a recipe that creates a soul-feeding meal that will sustain one for a lifetime, filling one with peace, power, gratitude, and happiness.

Consider though that the ingredients of this recipe are not easily obtained. Personal integrity arises out of deep self-knowledge and is nurtured by the willpower to unflinchingly abide by one's moral code. Mindfulness is gained from spiritual acuity that is gained in turn from long, methodical spiritual practice. Charity grows out of humility, self-sacrifice, and selflessness. Each one of these qualities involved in living a virtuous life demands self-discipline and a willingness to continually learn.

This book presupposes that all humans contain inherent goodness. Not surprisingly then, we all witness, and usually take for granted, countless daily acts of virtuous behavior toward one another throughout the world. The door held open for a stranger, the payment of another person's bill, the nod of greeting when passing, and so on. We can't help but to be nice to one another; we can't help but have the desire to help, because we are all children of God, and, being so, we all contain inherent goodness. The thing is though that the man who consciously chooses to live a virtuous life has taken these natural impulses to the next level. He refines his life through the regular use of personal integrity, mindfulness, and charity, making himself into a natural champion in his community. His "random acts of kindness" are not random, they are intentional.

Personal integrity, mindfulness, and charity will all be covered more in depth in later writings beyond this book. The reader will have the opportunity to engage in further learning about how to develop and practically use these skills. In the next chapter, we will discuss what it means to be a mature man living a virtuous life in today's world.

~ CHAPTER FIVE ~
Today's Self-Actualized Man

The term "self-actualization" was popularized in the mid part of the 20th century by the legendary psychologist Abraham Maslow. Self-actualization describes a human state of being where: a) all basic needs of life have been met and b) a person, through their mental and emotional development, has brought into reality (actualized) their life potentialities. This person is creative and spontaneous in life, happy and productive in their work, loving and stable in their relationships with family and friends, aware of their own strengths and shortcomings, high in self esteem, sensitive to justice and fairness in the world, and in touch with their own higher nature. "Self-actualization" is an entire school of thought and much has been written on the topic. For our purposes here I will focus on my own thoughts about what it means to be a self-actualized man today.

In my mind, a human being contains four fundamental quadrants of existence — the spiritual, the mental, the emotional, and the physical. Self-actualization occurs in all four quadrants. I will address each of these as they relate to a man's health and well being.

The spiritual quadrant. This dimension of a man, possibly more so than any other dimension, contains enormously broad parameters. For this book's purposes we will confine our thoughts to spiritual health as it is experienced by men in the mainstream culture rather than by men who choose the spiritual paths of the mystic or the ascetic.

First and foremost, it is important for a man to not confuse his spiritual life with his religion. Religions are human-made institutions that are defined by external constructs such as dogma, rituals, ceremonies, and codes of conduct. A man's spiritual life is wholly internal and is defined by an individual relationship with something larger than he: his Higher Power, his God.

Sometimes a man's religion and his spiritual life coincide neatly, and that man experiences few contradictions between the two. Many times, especially in men who are evolving spiritually, a man's religion and his spiritual life will contain contradictions that can be difficult or even impossible to reconcile. At such a divide, a spiritual man must determine for himself what the more important path to follow is: the promptings of deep intuition and relationship or the dictates of religious belief or dogma?

The spiritually self-actualized man will have developed both a keen awareness of the presence of universal truths operating in life and the use of important principles in living a healthy spirituality. This man has a fundamental understanding of how to use the greatest power in the universe, the power of love. He will be tolerant of others, non-judgmental in his outlook, forgiving of trespass, compassionate toward suffering, patient with his station and advancement in the world, mindful of his actions and his life habits, and intimately in relationship with his God. This man intuitively knows that he doesn't have the answers, that in all matters human things are more gray than black and white, that his expressions of love toward all creation are more important than any belief system to which he ascribes, and most crucially that he is a child of God. The man who embodies these truths is spiritually self-actualized.

The mental quadrant. We live in an age of intellectuality. Gone are the times when mythology, storytelling, and theology played as important a role in the world perspective as science. Now, in the modern world, science and the empirical method are the recognized harbingers and repositories of truth. But in today's self-actualized man, spirituality and intellect, myth and science closely blend with one another. This man's personal spirituality in large part guides his intellect. He knows to drink deeply from the well of collective wisdom, grounded in his psyche, when he contemplates any plan of action, any course of study, any creative endeavor.

On the mental plane today's self-actualized man has identified his own unique intellectual strengths (and weaknesses) and will put those strengths to work. This man knows his capacity to assimilate knowledge as well as his more refined mental processes. He has the foresight to know when an issue or a challenge is beyond his capacities, and he will seek assistance. He understands the difference between personal fortitude and needless, egocentric pride when he faces an intellectual challenge, and will conduct himself accordingly, not allowing pride to cloud his better judgment. He understands that engaging in academic pursuits that provide no direct benefit to the world are frivolous diversions of his intellectual talents. He understands that mental health is a state of mind rather than a rigid prescription of reality. The man who embodies these mental habits is intellectually self-actualized.

The emotional quadrant. In my view, emotions are the natural domain of the female, and rationality is the natural domain of the male. These gender distinctions are as old as humanity itself. When a human is conceived, its gender is unspecified. It is later in gestation, through a biological process, when sexual differentiation of the embryo occurs. Therefore, we all start out life with no gender, or both genders, if you will. At a fundamental chromosomal level males have a biological female component, and conversely females have a biological male component. It follows then that females have strong innate sources of rationality to draw upon, and males have strong innate sources of emotion to draw upon. The evidence is clear in my life that this is true. I know many women who are strongly rational, and many men who are well in touch emotionally.

Strangely, the experience in our Western culture has been that females are able to adeptly draw on their innate sources of rationality to balance out their natural state of emotion-based living, while males have, for many reasons, developed a cultural pattern of living stunted emotional lives. Thus, males in our culture often have no emotion-based inner dynamic to balance their natural state of rationality-based living. This puts men at a distinct disadvantage to women in terms of their ability to lead balanced healthy lives. Our world suffers as a result, as I have alluded to previously.

Today's emotionally self-actualized man does not experience such imbalance. This man owns his emotions; they are his friends and intimate companions. When a loved one dies or lies injured in a hospital bed, this man will shed the tears of his natural, healthy grief. When the sight of his life companion-to-be appears before him at the wedding alter, when the sound of his just-born child's first cries reaches his ears, when the reality dawns on him that through his own efforts and perseverance a life-long dream will come to pass, this man will shed the tears of joy and gratitude with no shame for the display. Sorrow, anger, shame, fear, joy, these basic feelings are no strangers to this man. He knows that his passion for life, for work, for relationship springs from these essential feeling states. His healthy emotional life and his intellect are what make him fully, beautifully human.

Today's self-actualized man either intuitively grasps his inner emotional life, or he has done the difficult personal work to learn how to access the inner life. Accessing that inner life includes a physical body component. Emotions can be physically felt in the body. Women know this fact intuitively, men don't. If a man is cut off from access to his inner emotional life, those physical sensations are deadened in his body. If he feels body sensations at all during emotional times, they often are felt in a disconnected way, rather than in healthy conscious awareness of them.

A self-actualized man makes the important connection between his emotions and what is happening in his body. His healthy body awareness tells him that his body is experiencing grief when grief knocks at the door. He feels where the grief is manifesting in his body — in his chest, in his gut, in his loins; wherever it is, he feels that bodily sensation. Rather than putting his shoulder to the door to keep it tightly closed, he opens the door to the grief and allows that emotion to fully come into his consciousness, and therefore into his body. When that happens, the man's consciousness and his body together experience the grief. The man can then fully embrace his grief, emotionally and physically, and move through the grieving into calmer waters, rather than shutting off his grief, which would allow it to grow and fester.

The self-actualized man understands the natural process of emotional expression that leads to calmness, peace, and emotional health. He has awareness of his choices regarding putting this natural process into play in any given situation, or not. He understands that there is a healthy balance between using emotional expression as a tool and

Chapter Five • Today's Self-Actualized Man 61

responsibly governing one's inner life. His emotions don't control him; he controls his emotions. He understands that emotions are not "good" or "bad," they just are. Emotions are rightfully acknowledged and honored for their contribution to a man's maturity. The man who embraces and honors his emotions is emotionally self-actualized.

The physical quadrant. The human body is a highly complex organism. I believe it is a miracle of creation both because of its anatomical and physiological complexity and because it is imbued with consciousness. This miracle called "the body" deserves regular close attention in order for it to remain vibrant and healthy for a normal lifespan, now approaching an average of 80 years in a man.

Today's self-actualized man attends to six parameters of physical health: nutrition, body movement (exercise), rest (peace in the body), medical oversight, personal hygiene, and intimate touch (sexuality).

Nutrition. Let's face it, most of us men in Western culture put unhealthy things in the body: refined sugar, red meat, alcohol, tobacco, etc. Fortunately, the body has amazing capacities to absorb, filter, and discard the toxic byproducts of such consumption. Proper nutrition plays a leading role in sustained long-term physical health; conversely, insufficient or improper nutrition is likely to be the single largest contributor to disease in humans. Proper nutrition is composed of a balanced intake of water, protein, carbohydrates, fats, fruits, vegetables, vitamins, and minerals. Plentiful advice on what these proper levels are abounds in the available literature, so we will spend no time on that here. Suffice it to say that the self-actualized man chooses to refrain from overindulgence in food and drink that do not contribute to nutritious sustenance.

Body movement (exercise). If the body is not put into regular motion, it will atrophy, just as the machine that sits idle and is not maintained will rust. If a man sits in his chair and only gets up to fetch something from the refrigerator or to relieve himself, his body will increasingly refuse to do his bidding when called upon. If that same man sits in his chair for only brief periods of rest and moves his body regularly, he will likely enjoy many years of energetic response from that body. Body movement can be categorized into two groupings: functional usage and recreational usage. The former includes activities such as walking, stretching, errand running, and working. The latter includes activities such as exercise, dance, sports, and yoga. The use of both of these groupings together contributes to healthy patterns of body movement. The self-actualized man does not allow sloth to rule his hours, and the primary defense against that demon is movement of the body.

Rest (peace in the body). Just as the body requires regular movement for healthy functioning, it also re-quires proper rest. Rest comes in several forms. The most common is sleep, or rest accompanied by loss of consciousness. Other forms of rest can be just as refreshing to the body: light napping and meditation (both involving rest with lowered consciousness rather than loss of consciousness, as

Chapter Five • Today's Self-Actualized Man 63

in sleep); controlled breathing, receiving massage, and lounging in spa or sauna.

Resting the soul also positively affects the health of the body, meaning to create time for the practices of active stillness and ceasing stress-producing thoughts and activities. Rest is covered in the faith traditions on the Sabbath, where one arrests the activities of the outer world and attends only to the soul during a day of non-engagement. The focus is turned inward; the soul and the body are then refreshed and rejuvenated, made ready again for the coming new round of external activity.

Medical oversight. Even though the healthy human body operates at an extremely high level of functioning, sometimes things do go wrong. The self-actualized man attends closely to his body, understanding that he alone is responsible for its proper upkeep. This man is strongly attuned to the messages his body sends him, and he takes appropriate action when warning signals come. Appropriate action involves doing the research necessary to uncover the root causes of his disease or disorder and then changing those unhealthy aspects of his life.

For example, a man may experience a frequent burning sensation in his chest after eating meals. He checks it out with his physician and discovers he has a stomach ulcer. What caused this condition? Is it the fact that at times he over indulges in fatty foods, or is it that he has tolerated a long-term toxic work environment such that it is now causing him a health problem? In either case, his body is telling him something is wrong and changes need to happen.

The self-actualized man takes appropriate action to relieve the disorder. He does not ignore the burning in his gut.

Personal hygiene. A clean house is a happy house. In conjunction with medical oversight, sound personal hygiene permits the self-actualized man to keep on top of a well-maintained body. Sound personal hygiene includes regular care of the skin, the hair, the teeth and gums, the hands and finger nails, the feet and toe nails, and the genitals. It involves cleaning all parts of the body, if not daily, then 2–3 times per week, grooming the hair on the head and any facial hair, keeping the nails trimmed, and brushing the teeth 1–2 times per day. It also involves wearing clean clothes and washing soiled clothes regularly, wearing appropriate footwear, and keeping body adornments to reasonable levels.

Intimate touch (sexuality). Touch is one of the five human senses. That being true, touch produces a lot of physical, emotional, and mental energy in a man. For those who choose a spiritual path of renunciation, the desire for touch is a condition to be overcome. For the rest of us, to live life without touch is to live life with severe disability, akin to what the blind or deaf experience. The importance of touch as a tool of communication amongst humans cannot be emphasized enough. When a man stands before another man and violently shoves that man, he is sending a clear message. When a man kneels before a child and embraces that child with a warm hug, he is sending a clear message. When a man stands before a woman and takes that woman in his arms to deliver a passionate kiss, he is sending a clear

Chapter Five • Today's Self-Actualized Man 65

message. Touch in the first example springs from aggression. Touch in the second example springs from altruism. Touch in the final example springs from sexuality. The desire for touch associated with sexuality in my mind poses the most challenge of any type of touch for a man. That point of connection can often cause a man to take actions he might otherwise not take, it is that powerful.

Humans are genetically programmed for reproduction. The seven billion humans alive on the planet provide ample evidence of this fact. All of the five senses come into play when the human reproductive instincts are engaged: vision, hearing, smell, taste, and touch. When a man fails to develop over time a positive moral code around his instinctual desires for intimate touch, all kinds of social ills can appear in his life: abuse, rape, siring of illegitimate children, addictions, etc. Other than the development of adult male maturity, this issue of proper control and expression of male intimate touch is likely the single largest challenge our male population faces in modern times.

Today's self-actualized man has achieved the maturity and awareness necessary to keep his desire for intimate touch in healthy perspective. He has discarded any boyish needs to reconnect with a mother figure. He refrains from objectifying women as purely vessels of pleasure. He is able to experience intimate touch with other men, in non-sexual ways, without fear or shame. He refuses to ever put himself in a position where he compromises his own moral code through inappropriate expressions of his sexuality. He pursues his desire for intimate touch with his female partner at appropriate times. He honors his God-given instinct for thrusting his masculine nature into the receptive feminine nature, thus recreating and sustaining a timeless, beautiful interplay between the sexes.

The desire for intimate touch can derive from goodness and be one of the most creative and affirming forces in the human repertoire. It can also derive from evil and be one of the most destructive forces in the human repertoire. The self-actualized man is fully aware of this dichotomy, and as in all other aspects of his life he chooses to march toward the good.

What I have just described regarding the manner in which today's self-actualized man experiences the four quadrants of his existence is a recipe for living life as a mature, noble man. Is this man a perfect creature? Certainly not. Few humans in recorded history have reached that divine state of existence. No, this man has his imperfections (they may be plentiful), and he has awareness of them when they surface.

Does every male walking the earth have the potential to create in himself a mature, noble man? I believe so. Today's self-actualized man has barely begun the journey of human potentiality. We can only imagine what that man will look like a thousand years in the future, just as men in the Middle Ages could only imagine what men have become today, in the 21st century.

∼

In the next chapter, we will explore the healing journey of one male, on his path to becoming a mature, noble, self-actualized man. It is quite a story.

～ CHAPTER SIX ～

A Hero's Journey

As mentioned elsewhere in this book, we have a huge problem in our culture today, one that involves our men. The problem is not about how our men outwardly behave or how they don't behave, it is about what is going on inside them. Many of our men today are walking time-bombs, and so all of us in the culture, men, women, children, elders, live and walk on a veritable minefield of male wounding. Millions of men today carry deep untouched and unhealed wounds from their boyhood days. Many don't know they carry such wounds; many are aware that they do, yet either way almost all of our men don't have a clue what to do about those wounds. Men who carry unhealed early-life wounds, whether they perceive them or not, and who do care for their loved ones and for the safety of the world often manifest the long-term effects of that wounding through self-destructive behaviors: ruined relationships, addictions, heart attacks, strokes, cancer, and, in the extreme, suicide. Men who carry such wounds who don't care about others or the safety of the world can bring physical and emotional violence to those around them: both friends and loved ones and even random strangers.

In either case we are dealing here with essentially a spiritual issue, an issue regarding disconnection from the deeper self, and disconnection from meaningful relationship with God. The unhealed wounds create a fundamental blockage, somewhat like what happens when cholesterol sticks to the walls of veins and arteries, plaque building up over many years that can create an environment for heart attack. What flows in the veins and arteries is life-giving blood; what flows in the deep parts of a man's soul is life-giving sacred energy. In both cases blockage can become so severe that the very existence of the man is threatened. It is true with the blockage of blood. It is also true with the blockage of sacred masculine energy. Medical science has made tremendous strides in healing heart disease caused by arterial blockage. Yet our culture still hasn't found a way to address the healing of soul wounds that block the flow of sacred energy in a man. Or has it?

Let's try on another story. This is a story of wound healing in a man. It is a story that repeats itself today in the lives of many men. These healing stories are few in number compared to the enormity of the problem involving our men in the culture. Nonetheless, the stories are present, and their magnitude is increasing amongst our men. Indeed, one of the main goals of this book is to create a cultural awareness for these stories. The tale about to be told shows that there is hope for all men to get the tools and support they need to heal their boyhood wounds, and to become whole and complete men. This is a story about a man named Jacob.

∽

Chapter Six • A Hero's Journey

The linoleum floor of the men's bathroom was cold and hard and felt unforgiving, but the door to the room could be locked, and then it was safe. Sitting at his desk in the office, not being able to focus at all on the work in front of him, Jacob was mired in grief. When the grief became so overwhelming that Jacob felt it rising to the surface and nothing he did could keep it in any longer, he would quietly head to the bathroom and lock the door and go to his knees, resting his forehead on the cold, hard linoleum, and let it come, wave after wave of grief, his sobbing silent so no one outside the room would hear him. He couldn't leave work; he needed the money too badly. He couldn't work; the grief kept him from being able to focus on anything. But he could go to this room at work; it became a temporary fortress against the world.

The trips to the men's bathroom were a common occurrence for Jacob during the winter of that year. That winter Jacob had lost his wife. She hadn't actually physically died, but it was just as bad for Jacob. Their marriage had fallen apart; the marriage had died. When Jacob's wife, Sarah, decided to move out of their home and get her own apartment, Jacob went into a severe tailspin.

Just two years before that Jacob and his wife had lost the family business and both of their livelihoods. They were forced to sell their house that they dearly loved. Sarah had moved on emotionally and let the loss go, but Jacob had not yet rebounded from the trauma and was living his life feeling little meaning and no purpose.

Jacob had tried to resurrect himself as an

entrepreneur but could not get anything going that would feed the family. The family financial security they had worked hard to build was crumbling. Sarah became more and more resentful of Jacob's inability to face his new reality. She took her issues to the internet and engaged in online relationships as a way of spiraling down herself. When Jacob discovered her activities months later, he confronted his wife, begging her to stop and go into marriage counseling with him. When she refused, Jacob gave her an ultimatum: either stop this behavior that was destroying their relationship and go with him to counseling, or move out and find herself. When Sarah chose to move out, Jacob's world came crashing down on him. On top of everything else that had happened, the loss of his marriage together with the woman he loved were too much for him. That loss brought him to his knees. Jacob was a broken man.

Unbeknownst to him at the time, that winter would bring the beginnings of a new life for Jacob. When a man finally arrives at the point of brokenness, when he finally hits his bottom, he then has a choice. He can either wallow in his mess or he can surrender. If he chooses the path of surrender, then good things can begin to happen. Getting to a place of surrender: this is a place most men find difficult to reach. That is true because the universally accepted attitude of men is to not surrender but fight.

Men are taught from early on in life to fight and to keep on fighting no matter how tough it gets. The measure of a man, to most men, is not whether he lives or dies but how hard he fights. For our fallen heroes, we reserve the phrase: "He fought the good fight." So if we are programmed at our deepest levels as men to fight, (to the death, if necessary), then how can the notion of surrender-so-that-life-can-begin-anew make any sense at all? That notion is so foreign to men that the mere mention of it makes us think of ourselves as something less than real men, as weaklings. The label that he is weak is just about the worst insult a man can receive. Men are supposed to be strong. Strong men fight; strong men do not surrender, ever. Weaklings do.

Jacob knew these things, knew them at a subconscious level. He never really consciously told himself, "I'm going to fight as hard as I can through all of this and never give up." He just knew it in his depths. He was not a quitter.

Not long before the business collapsed, Jacob was riding high. He had a thriving business. He was highly respected, a sought-after pillar of the community. He had a wife he loved and three children he adored. He owned an expensive, beautiful home, and his balance sheet was looking enviable. Then it all started to unravel.

Jacob at that time had the usual set of life challenges: problems in the business, problems in the marriage, and so on. Jacob viewed the problems as a normal part of life. He saw himself as a strong man, a man who fought to keep all the important parts protected and safe — his family, his business, his home, and his security. Jacob kept the faith that as long as he remained a good man at heart and did what he was supposed to do, as long as he worked hard and fought for what he believed in, then everything would be fine. It didn't work out that way.

Jacob had no idea that life with a capital "L" was going to show up. It all started when Jacob got word one day that major competitors were moving in to encroach on his business. Jacob had worked hard for 10 years to get his business running and successful, and it was finally paying off. Now this threat had come from out of nowhere.

Jacob went into fighting mode to save his business and gave it everything he had. Everything he had was unfortunately not enough. Many months later when the business was forced to close and Jacob saw his life's work destroyed, his heart sank, but he kept on fighting. So-called "friends" whom he thought he could count on disappeared when his business crumbled, but he kept on fighting. Jacob then had a hard time finding work, so he ended up hosting tables at a local restaurant, humbling duty after occupying the throne of his own little kingdom. Jacob's heart sank a little further, but he kept on fighting. Things deteriorated financially to the point that Jacob was forced to sell his dream home that he had worked years to acquire and move his family into an apartment. Jacob's heart sank yet more, but he kept on fighting.

And then the worst came, his life mate left. Jacob's heart had sunk so low that when his marriage unraveled and Sarah left him, he felt utterly bereft of all the underpinnings in his life: his passion, his dream, his business, his financial security, his reputation, his house, and now his beloved wife. It was too much. Jacob had no more fight in him. He

Chapter Six • A Hero's Journey

was defeated. So the only thing left he could do was get down on his knees, put his forehead to the floor, and weep. And weep, and weep.

Our reader might venture a guess as to who comes into the picture at this juncture in Jacob's story. Yep, that's right — the Big Guy, the Grand Poobah, the Man Upstairs. In the midst of Jacob's weeping, in his darkest hour, in his brokenness God shows up. God shows up because Jacob invited Him to show up. Jacob had a choice when life brought him to his knees. If Jacob continued to fight and struggle in his darkest hour, he would simply wallow in his mess, and God would let him wallow, loving him through it all but not rescuing him. If Jacob chose to surrender at this point, then he would open himself to receive God's Grace in his life, and the healing could begin.

Men who continue to fight when life circumstances have brought them down, who refuse to surrender, effectively shut themselves off from the healing energy of God's Grace. Any man who has experienced this kind of epic life journey and has come through it knows that there is a time for fighting, and there is a time for surrender. Those who only fight and never surrender tragically miss the true and lasting reward that surrender can bring. Jacob finally chose the path of surrender, after a tremendous amount of fighting with nothing to show for it but failure. That choice ultimately brought Jacob victory.

During his journey of grief and loss, Jacob experienced two separate and profound events that set him on a course toward permanent health and wholeness as a man. Both events landed in Jacob's life at precisely the moment they needed to. Both events caused Jacob to stretch far outside of his comfort zone. Both events were transforming for Jacob, in and of themselves. All Jacob had to do was say, "Yes" and then hang on for all he was worth. The winds of change took care of the rest.

Although he was making choices throughout this time of life, it felt to Jacob like the choices were almost being made for him, like some invisible hand was holding his and gently pulling him along. It all began with a conversation in Jacob's driveway between Jacob and his next-door neighbor. The neighbor and Jacob were friends. Jacob had been sharing the difficulties in his deteriorating marriage, and the neighbor could see the pain in Jacob's countenance.

Jacob was invited to church that day. He had many times seen the neighbor and his family leaving on a Sunday morning, and he missed those lost times with his own wife and children. In the driveway chat, he had expressed how he respected the neighbor family's habit of churchgoing, and that is when the invitation came. Jacob accepted the invitation and found himself soon after on a Sunday morning sitting in the pew with his neighbor. And then it happened, suddenly and without any warning.

Jacob could feel in church that day that his emotional cup was full to the brim. The choir was immersed in soulful harmony, praising God with enthusiastic song, hands clapping, piano and drums exclaiming. The joyful, reverent voices caused Jacob's quiet, stoic veneer to begin cracking. He hadn't consciously understood that this type of experience was just what he needed to shake loose the grief, but something much deeper in him did understand. That something showed up.

The tears came softly at first. Jacob was caught off guard. He could not make them cease no matter how hard he tried to bury them. His shoulders began to shake, and the shaking moved from his shoulders down into his body. Soon Jacob found himself sobbing uncontrollably, like at work, and he could not make it stop. Unlike at work, this was happening in front of people, in front of strangers. It was embarrassing. Jacob had never before in life showed any deep emotion like this in public. Now, there was no men's bathroom; no place to hide. Jacob felt completely exposed, naked to the world. Even so, he just could not stop the grief from coming any longer. The music from that choir had opened the flood gates.

Jacob felt his neighbor's arm around his shoulder, words coming softly and supportively: "Jacob, it's ok, it's ok." When his sobbing hadn't subsided after several minutes, the neighbor said to him, "Come with me Jacob," and led him from their pew to the front of the church. Jacob's friend gently guided him to his knees at the altar, and kneeling beside him with his arm around Jacob's shoulder and his head close to Jacob's, the friend began to pray. Jacob buried his head in his arms on the altar railing and let the sobs come full force. The surrender had finally arrived. Jacob could hold it in no more, could not fight any more. Life had won.

As Jacob let it go, let the grief consume him, he

felt hands being laid on his head, many hands. Jacob kept his head buried in his arms and allowed himself to be touched and embraced by the compassionate, healing energy of complete strangers. Years of stuffing and burying the pain and the grief had filled Jacob's cup; a lid of denial and stubbornness tightly covered it. Now those choir voices and those healing hands had gripped the lid on that cup and pried it back, allowing the eruption to occur. Jacob felt powerless to resist, so he didn't try. The visit to the altar lasted seemingly half a lifetime to him, but in reality the half hour he was there was a time of healing for many others who joined him. One man's uncorked grief opened the door for Spirit to flow. A congregation was blessed that day with much healing from a broken soul's surrender.

That day was a turning point for Jacob, but the Universe was not done with him just yet. Life circumstances came knocking, and Jacob had finally turned around and opened the door. He was raw, no longer with pretense, and there was work to be done. The Grand Sculptor was spinning His potter's wheel; the lump of clay called Jacob was beginning to take shape.

Also in these times of descent, Jacob found his way into counseling. The man who took Jacob's case was a licensed social worker, a man who had done much inner work himself. In sessions with the counselor, Jacob discovered several previously unrecognized pieces of his story. He learned that he had contributed much to the ruination of his marriage; that just because his wife was the one to end it didn't mean it was all her fault. He learned

Chapter Six • A Hero's Journey

that his wife was in an entirely different place in her life than where he perceived her to be — Jacob had been in severe denial. He learned that he was a stronger man emotionally and spiritually than what he perceived himself to be, and that regardless of this loss, life would go on. He didn't have to live continually with emotional devastation; he could heal; he could be just fine in time. Jacob learned that he had been emotionally dependent on his wife and had been unconsciously handing her his power for years, a novel concept to him at the time.

With all this self-discovery accomplished through many therapy sessions, Jacob still was not able to grasp his essence as a man. He could feel that something fundamental was missing. The counselor could empathize with Jacob's core struggle; the counselor had taken that very same journey. Jacob had come a long way, but there remained a great chasm still in front of him that he only dimly perceived. Jacob was still not awake.

One day Jacob came to session prepared to work on himself when the counselor spoke up: "Jacob, I want you to consider doing something. I think you are ready for this". The "something" was a men's training. Jacob's counselor had been through the training himself. He gave Jacob some literature on the sponsoring organization and described in general terms what occurred during the training. He avoided talking in detail about the experience, explaining that details were intentionally withheld so as not to bias Jacob's own personal journey through the event. The counselor asked Jacob to trust him. Jacob felt the counselor had earned his trust in their relationship, so he accepted the invitation and chose to attend the event.

Unbeknownst to Jacob at the time, he had just signed up to become a fully mature man. That concept was unknown to Jacob because he had simply never been exposed to the notion that there is a fundamental distinction between mature and immature men. Until this point in the story — through leaving home as a teenager, and then college and marriage and children and career and now severe loss — Jacob the man had not evolved beyond responding to the world and everything in it as an adolescent. He was stuck internally at age 18; he's 38 now. Worse yet, he's not even aware that he's stuck there. With gentle guidance from the skilled and compassionate counselor, Jacob was just beginning to glimpse that his entire frame of reference as a male was fundamentally stunted, that he was lost in it, that it wasn't working at all for him, and that life could and should be a lot different than he had been experiencing it for the last two decades.

So, he trusted his counselor and went. Jacob didn't have a clue what this men's training was about, but he did know that things in his life had to change. He remembered his counselor's admonition that, regardless of what happened, Jacob would be safe. Safety was not what Jacob was concerned about: peace of mind and solace from his suffering were foremost in his thinking. If a men's training could help bring him some answers, Jacob was willing to risk much, including his safety.

He arrived at the camp on a Friday evening and left to return back home two days later on a Sunday afternoon. During the 48 hours he was there, Jacob, along with two dozen other men, took a journey down into themselves. He and his fellow trainees were guided on this journey by 40 trainers, men who had each taken this same journey themselves previously, and who were present now because they all had an abiding passion to assist men in finding their maturity. Just like every other man there, both trainee and trainer, Jacob experienced his own unique personal journey. Jacob's was the hero's journey, the journey of male initiation.

The experience of male initiation contains several distinct phases, ordered in this manner: the removal of the male from his normal society; a guided spiritual and emotional descent into the dark places of his psyche; a symbolic reckoning with his mother and father, or the fundamental break with child dependencies; a trial to endure and survive; the ascent out of the darkness carrying a newborn mature masculinity — the man now beholden only to himself; and a reintroduction back into the male's normal society, into which the newborn mature man brings his sacred masculinity.

The hero's journey of male initiation has played out in the lives of countless millions of men throughout human history, and has now been largely lost in the modern Western world. Countless millions of men in the world today experience life as Jacob had experienced it up until the time of his initiation, as stuck adolescents living in full-grown bodies. Just as the healing experience in the church had dropped out of the clear blue sky in Jacob's life during his time of greatest grief and loss, so this men's training and Jacob's initiation journey came out of nowhere to help him find his way on a path of transformation and renewal. Jacob slowly gained the awareness that these seminal experiences had appeared in his life at the time they did for a specific reason, and that there was a beneficent Presence guiding this process. Jacob was coming into a place of openness, and humbleness, and forgiveness. He had begun to heal.

Things actually got worse for Jacob after he experienced these life-changing events. His grief deepened, and his very sanity was tested by his unfolding life story. Jacob's life continued to fall apart, and he continued to flounder from feeling lost and rudderless. But something fundamental had changed inside him. Jacob began to discover himself as a maturing man. He progressed through counseling. He became immersed in his newfound personal inner work. He slowly developed a meaningful relationship with God. He nurtured his children, and he forgave both himself and his former wife for all the mistakes in their marriage.

Jacob's essence as a mature, noble man began to unfold in his life. He started experiencing life in its fullness. He witnessed himself growing and changing mentally, emotionally, and spiritually. In his openness Jacob began to give himself more authentically to those around him, to speak more from a sense of personal truth, to give and receive support and love in non-judgmental ways, to embrace beauty and goodness in the world. Jacob had taken the hero's journey, had endured it, and in time had come out the other side to a place of inner peace. Through an act of surrender, Jacob had transformed himself into a whole and complete, mature, noble man. He was now in reality the man he never knew he could be.

～ CHAPTER SEVEN ～

Conclusion

Through the stories of Joey, Oro, and Jacob, I have presented several important concepts about what it means to grow up all the way as a man, and what it means to not do that. These stories are directed toward younger men, but really they speak to all men, no matter their age. A human male is never too young to begin the lessons of maturity and virtue, and never too old to wizen in these ways.

The hero's journey is a difficult one. It is supposed to be difficult. It is a dangerous pilgrimage because it involves wounding, and strife, and even death. The hero's journey is essential for a man to become whole and complete as a human being. This journey can happen in a man's life in many different ways and at any age. Regardless of the source or the catalyst, this journey holds the most fruit for those men who choose to be led through it by other men who have already made the trip. When he is guided by those who have already made the hero's journey, a man experiences initiation into the world of mature men.

The reader might ask: where can I go to experience my initiation into the world of mature men? Modern Western culture, particularly in the United States, offers few opportunities for men to do this. I was fortunate to find the necessary vehicle for my own journey. It came in the form of a training adventure. That event, something called the "New Warrior Training Adventure," is held many times a year around the world. It is conducted by The ManKind Project, a non-profit organization that exists to initiate men. If the reader feels ready to take the next step in his life toward his own initiatory experience, an organization like The ManKind Project is a primary source for helping to make that journey happen.

I have intended to offer a blueprint in this book for a man to begin that journey for himself. It is my belief that the hero's journey involves three phases: life before initiation, the initiation experience, and life after initiation. That third phase, life after initiation, can involve many years of personal inner work, if a man chooses to make the effort. I honor any man who chooses to make that effort. To the men who make that choice, working to evolve themselves into whole and complete men, I will offer additional writings on practical ways to bring their self-actualiaztion into existence. Coming soon will be small handbooks, each one devoted to seven major areas of life: spirituality, marriage, family, health, vocation, inner work, and life ministry.

My primary mentor in this work, Don Jones, teaches: the initiation of men is the hope of the world. I believe that. If you, the reader, have absorbed the learning in these words thus far, I suggest that you may now be ready for a major step in your life to occur. I challenge you to embark on your own hero's journey.

It takes courage.

Next man.

PARADIGMS

In thinking through the material for *The Male Manifesto*, I have drawn on numerous personal paradigms of life that have informed the writing in this book. These paradigms create an order to the universe that gives me hope and comfort, providing perspectives that give the reader guidance.

- God exists. God transcends all religions. God is far beyond all human comprehension in humanity as we know it now. God is the Universal power of love.

- Humankind is a special creation of God unlike any other life form on the planet. We are made in God's image. As true children of God, we have inside of us two special gifts: individual consciousness and the power of free will. Our species is on an upwards evolutionary curve. As sentient beings, we have not achieved our potential.

- The world is advancing; it is getting better. Contrary to popular thought and to the unconscionably negative messages put forth by the various forms of news and entertainment media, humankind is advancing. Average health quotients, and thus life spans, are increasing; infant mortality is decreasing. More people have nutritious food and clean water than ever before. Access to information has brought the world community closer. Advances in technology have brought enormous positive changes to all sectors of society. Pursuit of spirituality is on the rise; sectarianism is in decline.

- The institution of marriage, embattled as though it may seem, is actually poised for nothing short of a renaissance. Lowered marriage rates and higher divorce rates are indicative of the wide and deep cultural trend of people challenging the normative conceptions of what marriage should be. We are in the soul-searching phase of a new marriage paradigm.

- Today, a number of differing family structures exist in the culture, including the traditional "nuclear family," blended families, single-parent families, extended families, etc. The structure of family life is not all that important. What is important is that love for one another, and for the sanctity of the family, rises above all other conditions or philosophies of what a healthy family is. Jesus taught that a human is to love all other humans just as much as one loves God, as one loves self. This is nowhere more true than in family life.

- Marriage is a sacred bond. It is primarily a spiritual pact between two persons, at its purest endowed by God with divinely inspired power, and based on unbreakable friendship and fidelity. Marriage also has economic and sexual agreements and privileges, but in its essence it is a spiritual relationship.

- Men and women are undeniably, unequivocally, fundamentally different. No question about it. This is a good thing. Men are rationality based; women are emotion based. Men are outwardly oriented; women are inwardly oriented. Men are wired to go out to hunt, and bring home the bacon. Women are wired to build the nest, and care for the family. Yes, there are countless individual exceptions. On a macro level, across the expanse of the human species over thousands of millennia, gender differentiation is a universal truth. To deny it is mere foolishness.

- Women mature in a nature-based manner into adult females in all-important aspects of life — physical, mental, emotional, and spiritual. The primary mechanism for this nature-based maturation is physiological: the onset of menstruation. Women, at a fundamental biochemical level, experience a virtual birth/death/rebirth cycle through the menstrual reproductive process. That profound physiological experience guides women into maturity. Men, on the other hand, are not so fortunate. Men have no equivalent nature-based process that guides them into maturity. Thus, they must be socialized to it, or taught.

- Full maturity is not attained, with rare exception, by men until their mid-twenties; often much later. It is a mistake to view a young man prior to 25 as fully mature because the male human brain isn't grown until then, let alone the fact that most men in this culture have no access to formal maturity training, especially during the late adolescent stage of development. Just because a young man has reached the age of emancipation, holds a drivers license, can legally consume alcohol, and has possibly been through life changing circumstances such as marriage, child rearing, military service, or college doesn't mean he has reached full maturity. This is one of the most misunderstood and damaging societal dynamics present in our culture. How should men younger than 25 be expected to think and behave in mature ways when they are not fully physiologically capable of it yet and are not trained to do so by their elders? The short answer is: they shouldn't be.

- The essence of virtue, noble behavior and noble attitudes, is acknowledged by all world cultures, creeds, and religions. There are universal truths in the essence of virtue ; all primary scriptural texts worldwide espouse these truths. They include, but are not limited to, com-passion, treating others as one would treat oneself, fortitude and long-suffering, charity, self-love and self-respect, respect for the dignity of others, protection and caring toward the weak and infirm, tolerance, non-judgment, forgiveness, honoring the elders, non-violence, fidelity, honesty, non-covetousness, and love of

God. Living a virtuous life is a difficult path. It means sacrifice, making choices that often put others first, and mindfulness of one's actions.

- When a man has reached the state of living where he is able to embody the essence of full male maturity and the essence of virtuous behavior, many things happen. Such a man becomes a pillar, an example for those in his immediate circle. He becomes a man who attracts notice from others, whether they know him or not. For some he becomes a dangerous man. Such a man follows his own moral code as the foundation for all actions in life. Such a man is a fierce protector and a consistent provider, be it for his own family members, for the defenseless and oppressed, for his community, and even for all humankind.

- Fully mature, noble men are a rare commodity at the moment. They are hiding in the souls of all men. In many men, they are desperately crying out to break free. Fully mature, noble men are the salvation of our world.

GROUND RULES

My wish is that when using this series of handbooks the reader will understand and embrace several important, underlying ground rules. Mindfulness of such critical rules of personal conduct will center a man when putting the principles of maturity and virtue into daily practice. I view these rules as the foundational bedrock underlying the principles of The Male Manifesto. They are like the "good soil" that Jesus refers to in his parable of the seeds. The seven ground rules follow.

1. Judge not others on their own paths. As a reader of this book, you are presumably a family man or have intentions of being one. The way of the family man is not the only path for living a mature, virtuous life, nor is it the purest path. It is best to refrain from placing oneself in a position of moral superiority over one's fellow humans. Humbleness is like a cloak of shimmering gold for the mature, noble man. Leave the judging to God.

2. Always take the high road. Often the easy way is the way of criticism and blaming. The difficult path, yet the path most true to the principles of maturity and virtue, is the one that allows a man to seek common ground, to look for the best in others, and to strive for positive outcomes. When faced with adversity or attack from others, rise above them. Refrain from the all-too-human temptation of reacting to negativity: such

reactions produce only more negativity. Instead, respond to negativity using the wisdom that comes with maturity and virtue.

3. Seek balance in everything. The world has known many mystics who are also madmen, many business tycoons who are also social parasites, many artists who are also destroyers of culture. The mature, virtuous man is one who closely guards the integrity of all important aspects of his life, not permitting obsession in one arena to strangle health in others. Not only is he careful with balance in all aspects of his life, he actively seeks healthy interplay between aspects such as emotional life in relation to spiritual, physical health in relation to mental acuity, and so on. The idea is to nurture a fully integrated organism, and this is chiefly arrived at through balance.

4. Be true to yourself as a man. Own all of who you are, guard that ownership fiercely, and embrace your darkness as well as your light. Do not permit any other person to define who you are, what you feel, or what you believe. Until you take full ownership of your truth, you will remain a little boy, always seeking the approval of others. Mature men seek only the approval of the inner self. Virtuous men seek to make the Universal Truth and their own truth one and the same.

5. Be who you are. In a word, be authentic. Refrain

from manufacturing any reality that doesn't speak to you deeply. On the other hand, if it feels right, but you know it isn't right, don't do it. It does no one any good to live a lie, nor does it do anyone any good to live a truth that is damaging to self or others. Short of doing harm to self or others, if a trait, attitude, belief or behavior would be viewed as unpopular or unbecoming yet it springs from the deepest part of you, then wear it proudly as an important part of who you are.

6. Let go and allow life to flow. Do not attach to outcomes. Attach only to non-attachment. Very little is in our direct control. The only things I really can control are how I choose to believe and behave in any life circumstance. Outside of those, it all is in God's hands. The sooner this reality is accepted, the sooner comes calmness, joy, and serenity.

7. Find a way to forgive. There are few things more deleterious to the soul than holding a grudge. Refrain from giving any situation or relationship that much negative emotional energy. Forgiveness is the key, and that means finding a way to accept the offending situation where it is.

ACKNOWLEDGMENTS

In the writing of this book, I am grateful to a few gracious and caring men who gave of their time and talents to support the endeavor:

Don Jones, my primary mentor in men's inner work and initiation.

David Owen, a masterful writer who helped me shape content and form and contributed the art for the cover.

Bruce Carpenter, the man who crafted this book into a handsome artifact to hold.

FREDERICK MORGENSTERN

The Male Manifesto

Life as a Grown Man in the Modern World

Morning Star Press
Bloomington, IN
2020

© 2020 by Frederick Morgenstern

Morning Star Press

All rights reserved

Cover art 'Ridge Line' by David Owen
Cover and Layout Design by Allison Horner

The paper used in this book meets
the minimum requirements of
American National Standard for
Information Sciences—Permanence of Paper for
Printed Library Materials, ANSI Z39.48-1992.

Printed in the United States of America

ISBN 979-0-578-96853-7

www.ingramcontent.com/pod-product-compliance
Lightning Source LLC
Chambersburg PA
CBHW072013290426
44109CB00018B/2222